Harry Reeder's gifts of con
ary. This book is not only a
on the practical application

Reeder's urgent call to develop biblical leaders who are courageous, compassionate, and selfless is a battle cry to rescue our nation, our culture, and our churches from the suffocation of self-gratification.

Reeder is disturbed that churches have entrusted the world with defining what it means to be a leader. He tries to take that job back – and with it, he gives us help in knowing how we can develop and deploy those leaders in the church and beyond.

Drawing on a deep understanding of Scripture, a lifetime of ministry in the church, and a practical knowledge of military history, Reeder lays out clear biblical principles for success in spiritual leadership.

With compelling examples and practical suggestions, this book will challenge you to be a leader and to develop other leaders, and it will help you do both.

3D Leadership

Defining, Developing, and Deploying Church Leaders Who Can Change the World

by Harry L. Reeder III

MENTOR

Copyright © Harry L. Reeder, III 2018

paperback ISBN 978-1-5271-0156-2
epub ISBN 978-1-5271-0212-5
mobi ISBN 978-1-5271-0213-2

10 9 8 7 6 5 4 3 2

Published in 2018 and reprinted in 2022
by
Christian Focus Publications Ltd,
Geanies House, Fearn, Ross-shire,
IV20 1TW, Great Britain.

www.christianfocus.com

Cover design by
Daniel van Straaten

Printed and bound by
Bell & Bain, Glasgow.

CONTENTS

Introduction: The Multiple Dimensions of Biblical
Church Leadership. 7

Part 1: The First Dimension – Defining Leadership 11
   1. What Biblical Leadership is *Not*. 13
   2. Defining the Leader 29
   3. The Qualifications of a Christian Leader. 45
   4. What Makes a Leader Great? 57

Part 2: The Second Dimension – Developing Leaders. 73
   5. Thermometer or Thermostat?. 75
   6. The Example of the Greatest Leader 91
   7. The Church as a Leadership Factory. 105
   8. Five Habits of Multiplication Leaders. 121

Part 3: The Third Dimension – Deploying Leaders 135
   9. Past, Present, Future. 137
  10. Shepherds, Servants, Superintendents 151
  11. Fighting the Good Fight. 165
  12. Know Your Enemy 177

Conclusion: The Leadership Moment. 193
Acknowledgements 197
Embers to a Flame Ministry 199
Biographical Data. 201

Introduction

The Multiple Dimensions of Biblical Church Leadership

IMAGINE that you went to see a 3D movie but never got the special glasses they hand out in the lobby. You would be able to figure out basically what was going on in the film, but you would not be seeing it the way it was meant to be seen, and your eyes would probably begin hurting before long.

That is more or less what is happening with leadership in the church today. We have plenty of leaders, and new ones are being appointed all the time. But something doesn't look right, and sometimes it is downright painful to watch.

Why? The church used to be a leadership factory that developed leaders not only for the church but also for the world, and it also served as a distribution center that deployed those leaders throughout the world. But no longer – today it's the other way around. Most churches try to make leaders out of people who have been identified as successful in the world. But in most cases they are worldly leaders that have been influenced by a secular humanist worldview. In other words, today's church typically takes the leaders developed by the world and attempts to deploy them in the church, while thinking that a six-week leadership training class will undo what they have learned from the world and magically transform them into effective, faithful leaders for Christ.

One of the reasons for the current crisis is a distortion created when we focus too much on only one or two aspects of Christian leadership revealed in the Scriptures or ignore some of them completely. I want to show you from the Bible how the church can once again become a leadership factory and leadership distribution center for the world, by taking full advantage of all *three important dimensions* that God has provided and delineated for us in His Word. I call it '3D Leadership,' and it is a proven plan not only revealed in God's Word but also illustrated in the history of the church.

Why do I call it *3D Leadership*? Because Christian leaders are multiplied and mobilized when the church takes the time to *define* leadership, then *develop* leaders, and then *deploy* leaders.

If the church recovers this biblical leadership/discipleship effort, we know what will happen, because it happened in the first-century church! In Acts 17:6 there are thirteen words uttered by a frustrated pagan adversary of the Gospel and the kingdom of God as believers arrived in Europe. How I would love to hear those words once again – 'These people who have turned the world upside down have come here also.'

You and I both know *who* turned the world upside from Jerusalem to Europe in less than twenty-five years after the ascension of Christ – the Spirit of God through the people of God who comprised the church of God. We also know *what* turned the world upside down – the power of the Gospel. But the book of Acts also tells us *how* they turned the world upside down. The church embraced the initiatives of Gospel evangelism and discipleship; Gospel church planting and revitalization; Gospel deeds of love and mercy; and Gospel leaders defined, developed and deployed. These four Gospel initiatives were employed in every city as recorded in the book of Acts resulting in the Gospel expanding 'in Jerusalem and in all Judea and Samaria, and to the end of the earth.' This book will bring focus and clarity as to how we implement the fourth initiative of leaders being defined, developed and deployed not only in the church, but from the church into the world.

If I were to begin my pastoral ministry again tomorrow knowing what I know today, I would commit myself thoroughly to this 3D process of raising up Godly leaders: First, I would intentionally focus on *defining* with greater clarity the biblical concept of a

Christian leader. Secondly, I would invest more time and energy in *developing* leaders who are committed to that biblical concept of Christian leadership through life-to-life discipleship. And thirdly, I would make sure we are *deploying* them not only in the church and their families, but into every honorable sphere of influence throughout our culture.

> Whenever God decided to do something special, He called, equipped and empowered grace-driven leaders, who in turn multiplied themselves through other leaders.

If I could start my ministry all over again, I would certainly seek to be more consistent in intercessory prayer and more effective as an expositional preacher of the Word. And in fact, I cannot think of a single area of ministry where I would not desire to grow in faithfulness and competency. But the one thing that I would elevate on my priority list more than any other is 3D Leadership: defining, developing, and deploying Christian leaders who are capable of transforming society through a Spirit-filled, Christ-centered and Gospel-driven lifestyle, and who would intentionally multiply themselves by raising up the next generation of similar leaders.

One reason I would elevate leadership multiplication and mobilization is because this was a major priority and practice for our Lord Jesus in His three-year public ministry. Furthermore, the great movements of history in general and the movements of God's kingdom in particular have always been driven by the multiplication and mobilization of Godly, effective leaders. The Bible and other history books are filled with examples of this dynamic. Whenever God decided to do something special, He called, equipped, and empowered grace-driven leaders, who in turn multiplied themselves through other leaders.

We are living at a time when there is a tremendous opportunity for expanding the Gospel and the kingdom of God throughout the nations of this world. One contributing factor that has created this opportunity is a vacuum of good leadership and a simultaneous phenomenon of cynicism about today's leadership, created by the disappointing character of our present leaders and the failed concepts of secular leadership that have allowed them to gain and abuse power.

So let us return to the mandate, the mission, and the model of Christian leadership and intentional leadership multiplication found in the Scriptures. If our Lord grants us success, then the church will again become a leadership factory and distribution center. Join me in the following pages as we learn how our God can do this, through us, to extend His glorious kingdom, redeem lost men and women, and transform the cultural landscape of our world. And by God's grace and for His glory we may hear one more time, 'These people who have turned the world upside down have come here also.'

3D Leadership
Part 1

The First Dimension –
Defining Leadership

Chapter 1

What Biblical Leadership is *Not*

WHY do we do it?
Why do Christians want to learn leadership from the world's models when we know that 'worldly wisdom' inevitably conflicts with the Word of God and brings chaos and despair?

Genuine, effective leadership must be learned from God's Word, nurtured in God's church, and then transported into God's world. When this happens, we can anticipate a consistent reproduction of multiplication leaders who have themselves been transformed by biblical leadership. It is God's chain reaction. A transformed leader produces more transformed leaders – leaders who have been mentored within the church, then sent out to impact the world. By God's grace they will become His agents of change, and the process will continually repeat itself just as He intended. By faithfully applying the model of leadership revealed in the Scriptures, the church can again turn the world upside down (Acts 17:6).

At the moment, however, we are experiencing a cultural melt-down, and the church is partly to blame for it. Jesus said that God's people are the 'salt and light' to the surrounding culture, so when the church begins a free fall, all of American culture soon follows. Unfortunately the church is facing a self-inflicted death-spiral accelerated by the wrong kind of leadership.

Biblical Leadership is *Not* Self-Centered Materialism

What is the poisonous elixir that the contemporary American church seems so determined to consume? The answer is the worldly leadership model that is practiced and promoted in the boardrooms of American big business.

Is traditional American capitalism unbiblical and dangerous? No, I do not believe that *traditional* capitalism is the problem. But the leadership model that is infecting the church today – with disastrous results – is a product of *contemporary* capitalism, which is a greed-based, wealth-consuming mutation that has replaced the historically, Christian-influenced system of capitalism that created the wealth upon which our nation has thrived and blessed the world. Today's self-promoting corporate leadership is a deadly infection that countless churches are contracting as they thoughtlessly imbibe in the seductive potion of contemporary business models.

The benefits of Christian capitalism

Christian capitalism helped to shape our nation in a powerful, positive manner. The fresh influence of the Protestant Reformation spilled into the English colonies of America, forging their law and culture based on the Judeo-Christian worldview. Our nation was founded on that biblical consensus and flourished with it for over two hundred years, until the American worldview shifted to secular humanism in the late twentieth century. The biblical worldview is that God has authority over all things, and that pleasing Him should be the foundation of every endeavor. Secular humanism says that man, not God, is the final authority and that everything exists for personal pleasure and affluence.

Historically, the influence of Christianity on American business philosophy produced a huge and generally prosperous middle class that provided economic and cultural stability for the nation. Generally speaking, this traditional American capitalism was based on a lofty ideal – that corporate success is not the *consumption* of wealth but the *creation* of it. It was not greed that was good but doing good was good. The foundational ethic of traditional American capitalism – as influenced by Christianity – was not simply to 'do what is good for business' but to 'make it your business to do good.'

Throughout past ages, American capitalism was marked by extraordinary business leaders who also excelled as philanthropists by creating jobs, investing in the community, assisting the needy, providing meaningful public service, supporting the church, and making communities better in many other ways. Certainly there were a number of greedy business leaders, but they were marginalized, and certainly were not celebrated as they are today. Formerly in our country, God's people – the church – influenced American capitalism to practice a biblical model of servant leadership. Today, however, contemporary capitalism is influencing the church to practice a model of self-absorbed leadership. At one time the church produced effective servant leaders for the business world. Today the business world produces self-promoting leaders who are polluting the church.

The dangers of humanistic capitalism

Just as a biblical worldview affected all aspects of culture for most of American history, secular humanism today influences our bedrock institutions: law, government, education, healthcare, media, the arts, and the business community. The repackaged paganism embraced by contemporary American capitalism has rejected the influence of biblical truth in order to embrace a leadership model that promotes self-worship. Yet – alarmingly – much of the American church today is either thoughtlessly or pragmatically employing the humanistic model of contemporary capitalistic leadership. This model is not only unbiblical – it is ultimately destructive.

The evidence of this downward spiral in contemporary corporate America has been manifested by entire corporations faltering and closing, not because of problems on the 'ground floor' but because of moral failures in the top executive offices of leaders acting out their personal quests for wealth and power. This has produced a staggering loss of jobs, obliteration of countless individual retirement packages, untold numbers of divorces and wrecked families, widespread erosion of respect for the business community, and a general loss of trust in the American free-enterprise system.

Business leadership today is too often not about *leadership* but about the *leader* – his or her power, portfolio and profits. It is rooted in self-absorbed concepts of success, ego-driven desires for power, and what is now a socially approved form of greed that a century ago would have been decried as evil. This man-centered model of leadership is promoted anew every semester through collegiate MBA programs. American educational institutions are the front line of the culture war, and the typical university is militantly intolerant of any idea that would propose ethical absolutes in any degree program. Few university MBA programs today instruct future business leaders in the traditional, biblically-based ethic of sacrificial servant leadership, and only a pitifully small number of them even have a course on business ethics. Traditional American capitalism, along with the Judeo-Christian worldview on which it was based, is fiercely rejected in today's typical university.

What is being taught instead? That pragmatism rules. The end justifies the means. Ethics are not absolutes to be obeyed, but obstacles to be overcome. And now this humanistic, greed-driven model of leadership is being adopted and absorbed by churches throughout our nation. Yet greed destroys, so this popular new model of corporate leadership will eventually cripple the American church if it continues to be the primary source of our models and principles.

> At one time the church produced effective servant leaders for the business world. Today the business world produces self-promoting leaders who are polluting the church.

Selfism in the church

Take a close look at what passes for leadership training in many American churches and evangelical ministries.

First, promoting personal self-esteem is seen by many as a key goal of the church. But a self-centered life is exactly the opposite of Christ's call to a God-centered life and the essence of true Christian leadership, which demands a servant's heart and sacrificial actions. Today's focus on self-esteem did not come from Scripture, but from the narcissistic preoccupations of our culture. The 'It's all about me' philosophy prevails. Disturbingly, Christianity is being repackaged and redefined in a way that fits better with popular psychology.

This love of self, which is condemned by Scripture (2 Tim. 3:2), is deeply embedded in contemporary American culture, and sadly has infiltrated the church. We now have a generation of church members – and leaders – who are encouraged to constantly ask questions about themselves: 'How good do *I* feel about myself?' 'How good do *you* make me feel about myself?' 'How good does the *church* make me feel about myself?' And, by the way, 'How good does *Jesus* make me feel about myself?' The church has succumbed to the secular, cultural pressure of promoting self-esteem, instead of sharing the Gospel call to die to self through a God-centered life. If you miss the Gospel-driven Christian life, it is impossible to produce effective Christian leaders.

The counterfeit leadership training prevalent today also encourages an idolatrous preoccupation with physical and material prosperity. The salvation offered by Jesus Christ has been perverted into a 'prosperity Gospel,' which promises believers that they will become healthy and wealthy if they only 'confess it and possess it,' 'name it and claim it,' or 'believe it and receive it!'

Where did this perversion of Christianity come from? Certainly not the Bible. God does promise that He will supply all our needs (Phil. 4:19) and, 'I can do all things through Him [Christ] who strengthens me.' (Phil. 4:13) But in the verses right before that Paul says: 'I have learned in whatever situation I am to be content. I know how to be brought low, and I know how to abound. In any and every circumstance, I have learned the secret of facing plenty and hunger, abundance and need.' And earlier in the book he talks about having joy even in the midst of suffering: 'Even if I am to be poured out as a drink offering upon the sacrificial offering of your faith, I am glad and rejoice with you all.' (Phil. 2:17) He also says: 'for to me to live is Christ.' (Phil. 1:21) So God does not promise health and wealth to us in this life, and that which He does provide is so that we can use it for His glory, not merely for our own pleasure and personal fulfillment.

Through the self-absorbed teaching now dominating many churches, the true Gospel of grace is being blasphemously perverted. The result is that most Christians in contemporary culture have no concept of the biblical call to embrace suffering, sacrifice, and self-denial – which is not only an inevitable part of the Christian walk but is actually a gift and calling from the Lord. As Paul also says in Philippians: 'It has been granted to you that for the sake of Christ you should not only believe in Him but also suffer for His sake' (1:29). When such basic elements of Gospel life are denied or ignored, how can the church possibly respond effectively to the challenges of today's world, and how can it develop leaders who sacrificially serve others?

As misguided church leaders follow a worldly, self-directed model of leadership, the spiritual depth of believers and the stability of their local churches are steadily eroded. In the pulpit, 'tips for living' talks now replace Gospel-driven and Christ-centered sermons. Personality trumps character, and happiness trumps holiness. Perception becomes reality, and the sacred calling of Divine worship is replaced by personal entertainment. The congregation becomes an audience of spectators at the corporate gatherings of the church. They enjoy a 'worship experience' provided by the preacher and worship leaders who are the primary actors with God playing the role of the set-up man. Not long ago this would have been called blasphemy. Today we call it 'seeker-centered worship'.

In contrast, true worship has an audience of One – the triune God. But not only does He receive our worship, He enters into it by providing the presence and power of the Holy Spirit who enables us to worship with passion and sincerity. Too often today the biblical mandate to 'worship the Father in spirit and truth' (John 4:23) is being replaced with a self-directed question: 'How did that worship experience make me feel?' The result is that the Divine service of worship has now become the human service of entertainment, and the focus is on the worshiper rather than the One who should be worshiped.

In reaction to that worldly trend, other congregations have descended into thoughtless traditionalism, devoting themselves to comfortable, traditional worship practices with a fierce exclusivity that unwittingly promotes form over substance. That is also a man-centered extreme. In fact, the leaders of many such churches refuse to even consider new elements or styles in worship because they are afraid of the criticism and opposition they would experience from people who value tradition more than Scripture, and outward observance over sincerity of heart.

Knowing how to worship God in spirit and truth, while embracing seekers, teaching new believers, and encouraging mature Christians, requires Godly leadership and is necessary to produce more Godly leaders. Godly leaders are grown from the Word of God and empowered by the Spirit of God as an inevitable result of God's grace. They will not be raised up from the corporate model of leadership that has been baptized into the church. So to regain a biblical vision of leadership we must first retake lost ground by repenting of the plague of selfism that has infected the church. We must turn away from man-centered preoccupations and surrender to God's model of leadership found in Scripture.

Biblical Leadership is *Not* Cultural Accommodation

The church, and each Christian in it, is commanded to be 'in the world' but not 'of the world' (John 17:11, 16). Neither part of that commandment is easy. It is a real challenge to effectively follow Christ in the world around us, especially in a contemporary American culture where Christians are considered an irrelevant minority in an increasingly hostile environment. And in this technologically-enhanced information society it is also increasingly difficult to keep from being conformed to the world around us (Rom. 12:2).

One aspect of our God-created makeup is our inherent desire to fellowship with one another, and part of our sinful human nature is to constantly seek affirmation from each other. The ever-present temptation is to think that being loved by Christ is not sufficient and that we must have approval from others. This compulsion is so strong that it can often drive us to become man-pleasers rather than God-exalters.

> As misguided church leaders follow a worldly, self-directed model of leadership, the spiritual depth of believers and the stability of their local churches are steadily eroded.

The church on cultural steroids

Much of today's leadership in the church may be well intentioned, but is doomed to failure. Why? Because it has descended into cultural accommodation propelled by the desire for the world's affirmation. In today's culture 'God' is in, but Jesus is out; spirituality is in, but Christianity is out; religion is in, but the Gospel is out. In fact, Jesus, Christianity, and the Gospel are more than 'out,' they are scandalous. A desire for affirmation from the contemporary culture has led to redefining of Jesus as a therapist or consultant, faith as a means of personal success and self-promotion, and the Gospel as a self-help guide filled with pop psychology.

Many of today's church leaders are afraid to swim against the swelling tide of cultural opposition and even worse, they are compromising the essence of the Gospel and the call of the church to cultural transformation. They have lost confidence in the power of the Word of God, and specifically the Gospel message. Out of their fear of rejection and desire for popularity, these leaders have injected the church with cultural steroids to make it 'relevant,' hoping that people will be more likely to accept Jesus and that the church will become bigger and stronger and therefore more influential. But think about what happens to athletes in the sports world when they resort to the quick fix of steroids in their desire to be stronger or faster: they get the desired results initially, but at a great risk to their health and long-term success.

Likewise, allowing the culture's driving values into the church may temporarily inflate the numbers in the pews, but they move congregations toward spiritual destruction. 'There is a way that seems right to a man,' as Proverbs 16:25 says, 'but its end is the way to death.' Like the body of an athlete, the body of Christ may gain immediate embellishments of size and acclaim when injected with the steroids of cultural accommodation, but worldly leaders have actually introduced disease and eventual death into the body of believers they lead.

Of course we want to effectively communicate the Gospel within our surrounding context – whether our congregation is in Kenya or Kansas – but we must be determined not to substitute cultural accommodation for biblical faithfulness in the name of contextualization and missional effectiveness.

Pitching our tents near Sodom

The Bible gives us many examples of cultural accommodation and its inevitable failure. Consider Lot, who was apparently a well-intentioned believer (2 Pet. 2:8). First he 'moved his tent as far as Sodom' (Gen. 13:12). Then we later read that he is 'dwelling in Sodom' (Gen. 14:12). Eventually he is found 'sitting in the gate of Sodom' (Gen. 19:1), which apparently meant that he had become a city elder. The insidious siren call of Sodom's culture gradually conformed Lot and suffocated his witness. When he finally spoke up on behalf of his angelic guests, the disrespect of the city population surfaced with a vengeance and revealed a vehement hatred for the compromised man who had lost any witness, and he became an object of ridicule.

Notice that not only did Lot's accommodation fail to influence the surrounding culture, but he also lost the respect of his fellow citizens. That is obvious from the way the Sodomites mocked and threatened him when he sought to protect the visiting angels whom God had sent to rescue him and his family (Gen. 19:4-11). Instead of acting as the biblical light of the world, he was thoroughly assimilated into the secular culture – with no positive results. Rather than transforming the culture around him, he and his family became conformed to it.

That same phenomenon is happening in the American church today. In the name of cultural relevance, many congregations have been guided by their leaders to cross the line into cultural accommodation. They have pitched their tent near Sodom. In fact, some church leaders have bought a house *in* Sodom, thinking that they are making the church and its message relevant, when the opposite is true. But like Lot, church leaders who choose worldly models of leadership will eventually suffer a loss of respect and voice, and so will their churches. Along the way – even while perhaps gaining numbers – these wayward church leaders will have also compromised their ability to equip their members, who will fall into personal conformity to the world. How tragic this inevitable consequence is for the members of the church and their families!

The local church should be witnessing to the world without becoming like the world, and there is a pressing need for leaders who will set the pace. Cultural accommodation is easy today. Long gone is the day when the Judeo-Christian worldview dominated our culture, encouraging people to do what was right and discouraging what was wrong. Living daily for the Lord is harder than ever in America. Passionate and faithful Christians are swimming against the cultural current on a host of issues, which include not only public policy ones like same-sex marriage, the sanctity of life, and the loss of religious liberties – but also with issues that are more 'up close and personal' in their daily lives.

Sunday worship or worshipping sports?

A group of parents in my church came to me with a real-life dilemma that might not have made the evening news, but was extremely important to them. It was also typical of what American believers and their families are battling today.

'Pastor Reeder,' they explained, 'we want to honor the Lord's Day, but our children's sports programs are on Sunday morning.'

We sat down and I listened to their story. Their local recreation league scheduled practices and games on Sundays, so they wondered: Should their families skip worship during the season? Should they pull their kids off the teams? Eventually they decided, appropriately, that obedience to Scripture and family worship on the Lord's Day was far more important than sports. That may seem like an obvious choice to some readers, but it is not the norm. With the prevalence of child-driven families in today's culture, it takes courage and conviction to make the right decisions – the kind of courage and conviction that church leaders must model if they desire to disciple and shepherd members and their families.

As I led these parents through the Scriptures toward a resolution of their problem, I thought about my own childhood in the American South of the 1950s. We had some significant cultural issues that needed to be addressed in that time and place, but having to choose between Sunday worship and ball practice wasn't one of them. In fact, sports programs not only avoided activities on Sundays, but would not even schedule practice or play on Wednesday nights when midweek church services were routinely held. Why not? Was the culture of the 1950s more sensitive to the worship and prayer schedule of the Christian church? Certainly it was, to a degree, but that wasn't the main reason that teams avoided Sunday and Wednesday night practice and play.

The main reason was that they would not have had enough players to do anything if the committed Christians were absent. *And most of them would have been absent.* Christians connected in the society by playing in the community leagues of the day, but they also prioritized biblical obedience and commitment to Christ's church and Lord's Day worship. In response, the surrounding culture was affected by their faith and was shaped by it. Church leaders of the day taught that the Lord's Day was sacred – a gift from God – and was an essential means of grace in the life of a Christian. Under the influence of biblically-based leadership, most Christians observed the Lord's Day with worship, rest, and being with their families. And unlike today, the parents' need for the child's friendship did not trump their call to be parents and choose the right priorities, even if it did not meet their child's approval. They didn't toss all of that aside to play ball. And if the Christians didn't show up, the ball teams couldn't function. Therefore, the athletic leagues adjusted their schedules to accommodate believers, rather than the reverse.

Not so today, and the cultural accommodation by the church actually lessens our opportunity to impact the surrounding culture. Yes, some church leaders would argue that such accommodation enhances evangelism. But please remember that true effectiveness is never achieved at the expense of faithfulness! When a child's desire to play ball becomes more important to Christian parents than Sunday worship, the local church and its leadership are failing. The family is being discipled by the culture instead of being discipled by the church. We do have a mandate to connect with the surrounding culture, but we must do so through obedience to God's Word, not disobedience. Remember, we are called by our Lord to be '*in* the world' but 'not *of* the world'. Thoughtless accommodation to the world eventually becomes *capitulation*, and our witness for the Lord is rendered useless.

> The local church should be witnessing to the world without becoming like the world, and there is a pressing need for leaders who will set the pace.

Biblical Leadership is *Not* Reactionary Traditionalism

On the other hand, church leaders must not overreact to the trend of accommodation by plunging down the equally slippery slope of traditionalism. The reactionary trend of making the local church a museum of past achievements is equally unbiblical and ineffective. The church is to be a movement of the kingdom of God transforming the present and changing the future, not a monument of religious nostalgia.

Think about it this way: A man decides to keep his boat in a shed all the time because he doesn't want it to sink. He's right – the boat won't sink if it stays in the shed. But it's also absolutely useless as a boat. If the church is taken completely out of the world in an attempt to avoid compromise, it may not be guilty of accommodation, but – like the boat – it will be useless.

Sometimes we need to be reminded that although Jesus said we should not be *of* the world, He does want us to remain *in* the world. In fact, He actually prayed, 'I do not ask that you take them out of the world' (John 17:15). And sometimes traditions that are not biblical need to be challenged and even upended for the good of the church. A conversation I had recently is an example of this...

'Where is your church?' a new acquaintance asked me.

'I don't know,' I replied honestly.

'Huh?' he said, puzzled. 'How can you not know where your church is if you're the pastor?'

'Well, I do know the location where our church meets,' I explained. 'But as to where the church is right now, I don't know. Some of it may be at school. Some may be at a shopping mall. Or at home. Or maybe traveling – in cars, in airplanes. Some are all over the country, and a few are even in other parts of the world.'

My point – which my new friend quickly grasped – was that according to the Word of God, the church is not a building. It is the people of God who gather to worship Him, and they are all over the place, engaged in lifestyle evangelism and disciple-making. Our congregation meets in a certain location at various times, but *the members* – not a structure of brick and mortar – are the church.

Just like the church should not be confined to one particular location, we do not want it to be enslaved or limited by traditions that come more from human preferences than Divine principles. Such traditionalism can give churches an identity that is far different than the one Christ intended for His beloved bride. 'We've never done it that way before' can sometimes be a straight-jacket that keeps the Holy Spirit from doing great things in the way God wants to do them.

God's Path to World-changing Church Leadership

We must avoid sliding down the treacherous slope of accommo-dation on one side and the equally dangerous slope of tradition-alism and isolation on the other. Instead, God calls us to live and minister at the pinnacle – the point of tension – where God's truth is lived and proclaimed in love. We can't achieve this on our own; it requires knowing the Word and trusting in the power of the Spirit of God.

That is where biblical leadership does the Lord's work: pro-claiming the Gospel and making disciples according to the Word and through the Holy Spirit. Remember, God's transforming grace meets people right where they are. Nobody has to 'get better' to come to Jesus. This glorious truth of Scripture is summarized well in the words of the great hymn: 'Just as I am, without one plea, but that thy blood was shed for me.' Another classic, 'Rock of Ages', affirms the same truth when it says: 'Nothing in my hands I bring, simply to thy cross I cling.' And praise the Lord, when we come to Him just as we are, He will never leave us as we are. We're saved by faith alone, through grace alone, in Christ alone – but because of the love of Christ, faith and grace never remain alone in the child of God. When those whom God has saved are enabled through biblical leadership to grow by grace, then the transforming power of the Gospel at work within us and upon us will flow from our lips and our lives, attracting and drawing men and women from the world to Christ and His kingdom as we 'seek to save the lost' (Luke 19:10).

God's grace is glorious, all-powerful, and as another hymn declares, 'greater than all our sins'. It not only redeems sinners but transforms them. Grace-filled leaders will become transformed leaders, and then inevitably will become transformational leaders. Committed to true evangelism and disciple-making, they will unleash God's church as a change agent in the surrounding society. It happened with Moses, David and Paul, and it can still happen today as we *define, develop*, and *deploy* such leaders in the church and send them into the world.

The transforming power of the Gospel changes men and women. When they change, their families change. When families change, their neighborhoods change. When neighborhoods change, cities change. When cities change, nations change. And when nations change, the world is turned upside down.

Let's begin here and now. We live in a new dark age. Yet, we must remember that light shines most brightly in darkness. We have a great opportunity before us to bring light back into our darkened nation. To do so, we must put aside the false promises of self-centered materialism, cultural accommodation, and reactionary traditionalism. We must embrace and employ God's methods for leadership definition, development, and deployment. In our present darkness, let there be light – the light of the Gospel of Christ shining forth from His church like a 'city set on a hill' (Matt. 5:14).

How do we get there? The answer is actually astoundingly simple. Christ, in His three-year ministry, gave us the initial ministry paradigm as He intentionally prioritized defining, developing, and deploying leaders who wquld amazingly impact a hostile and pagan world through Gospel evangelism and disciple-making. Then those leaders produced others like them, taught us more about the process in the New Testament epistles, and turned the world upside down. In the next chapter, we will learn more about how the Bible defines such 'world-shaking' leadership.

Questions for Thought and Discussion

1) What are some examples of self-centered materialism mentioned in the chapter, and what are some others that you have seen in the church today?

2) How does 2 Corinthians 12:1-10 relate to the 'prosperity Gospel,' which teaches that God promises health and wealth if only we have enough faith to claim them? What about James 4:13-16?

3) How does the Apostle John define 'worldliness' in 1 John 2:15-17, and what are some ways that your church, and you personally, could be tempted to fall into it?

4) What's wrong with people saying 'We've never done it that way before' when discussing suggested changes to a church, and what can be done to prevent or correct such an attitude?

5) How can God use this book in your life, and in your church? Take some time to pray that it would be a catalyst for revival and reformation.

Chapter 2

Defining the Leader

WHO was the target audience for the Sermon on the Mount? The five thousand? You? Me? All of us? Each of those answers is correct, in a way, because the Holy Spirit has been changing hearts with those words ever since the Lord spoke them.

When Jesus delivered His Sermon on the Mount, however, He was speaking first to His disciples. Matthew introduces the Sermon on the Mount with these words: 'Seeing the crowds, [Jesus] went up on the mountain, and when he sat down, his disciples came to Him. And he opened his mouth and taught them.' (Matt. 5:1-2) The Sermon on the Mount was a training class, and it was directed first to the twelve leaders whom Jesus had chosen. Obviously, He was aware of the multitudes on the hillside listening to Him, but the primary target audience was the Twelve.

In fact, if you carefully study the life of Christ in the Scriptures, you'll see that a majority of His time and energy was spent on leadership development. He focused heavily on training three specific groups of leaders. He defined leadership for them, developed them as leaders, and then – at His ascension – deployed them into the world.

Who were the three groups? You can see them clearly in the Gospels: the Seventy, the Twelve, and the Three. Jesus defined leadership for them by 'doing and teaching'. He developed these people as leaders through discipling them, and then He deployed them into the world. Within a quarter of a century the civilized world would be turned upside down by them.

In this chapter, we will focus on the meaning of biblical leadership by first making some general observations about the Leader of all leaders, and then we'll discuss a very specific definition that arises from Christ's example and teaching.

An Incarnational Leadership Model

When the Lord Jesus Christ came into this world, He took upon Himself a physical body, and God became a true man. In that body He was fully God and fully man, and in that body He went to the cross to redeem His people, to defeat Satan and the principalities of darkness, and to purchase a triumphant church. In fulfilling this mission He simultaneously displayed a model of leadership and implemented a strategy for leadership multiplication. This is the model of leadership that the American church needs today – a model that if implemented will impact the world. Almost two thousand years ago Jesus initiated the model of 3D Leadership – He *defined*, *developed*, and *deployed* leaders who in turn repeated the same model, and in less than a generation the known world was turned upside down.

The model at work in the first century

Think more about what Jesus did as heaven's Champion, our Redeemer, in fulfilling His threefold incarnation mission. First, He came into the world to save sinners: 'She will bear a son, and you shall call His name Jesus,' the angel said in Matthew 1:21, 'for he will save His people from their sins.' Paul also writes: 'The saying is trustworthy and deserving of full acceptance, that Christ Jesus came into the world to save sinners.' (1 Tim. 1:15) Secondly, He came to destroy the works of Satan – the principalities and powers of darkness. 'The reason the Son of God appeared was to destroy the works of the devil,' according to 1 John 3:8. And Jesus' third missional objective was to purchase a church that would be victorious over sin and Satan – as Ephesians 5:25-27 explains: 'Husbands, love your wives, as Christ loved the church and gave Himself up for her, ... so that he might present the church to Himself in splendor, without spot or wrinkle or any such thing, that she might be holy and without blemish.' We also see this mission of Christ in Paul's address to the Ephesian elders: 'Pay careful attention to yourselves and to all the flock, in which the Holy Spirit has made you overseers, to care for the church of God, which he obtained with His own blood.' (Acts 20:28)

Saving sinners, destroying the works of Satan, establishing His triumphant church on earth, and essential to achieving His goals was the strategy of leadership multiplication. Satan is well aware of the priority Jesus places upon this, so he not only attacks the worship and ministries of the church but he also attacks its leadership. That's why the Apostle Paul warned the elders at Ephesus in this way: 'I know that after my departure fierce wolves will come in among you, not sparing the flock; and from among your own selves will arise men speaking twisted things, to draw away the disciples after them.' (Acts 20:29-30)

The victory of Christ in fulfilling His mission was declared at the resurrection, the Great Commission was initiated at His ascension, and the result of His model for leadership and leadership multiplication was that the world was 'turned upside down' (Acts 17:6) in about twenty-five years. You can almost feel the frustration of the man who uttered those words in his analysis of what had happened through the power of the Gospel, the Holy Spirit, and the implementation of Christ's model of leadership multiplication. During those early years, it had an impact unlike anything else that ever happened in the history of humanity, and that was only the beginning.

Untold numbers of people have been transformed from spiritual death to life by the Gospel of Jesus Christ. Nations have been established, reformed, and some even toppled by its impact. Political and economic systems have arisen, undergone refinement, diminished, or disappeared because of its influence. Missions and other ministry movements have transformed lives and cultures throughout the world and through the ages. The Gospel, advanced by Christ's model of leadership, has reverberated throughout history, so much so, that the Western world has divided time into B.C. and A.D. – 'before Christ' and *anno Domini* ('in the year of the Lord'). Meanwhile, the church of Christ has, by the grace of God, withstood widespread rejection, persecution, mass martyrdom, internal failures, and unfaithful followers.

If a human world leader or a multinational corporation tried to affect the world in even a comparatively minor way today, consultants would be summoned to develop an international marketing strategy. A worldwide database would be constructed. Mass media would have to be deployed, including advertising campaigns, multimedia marketing tools, news media liaisons, websites, branding, direct mail – all of man's methods of modern communication. But that's not what Jesus did. In fact, Jesus repeatedly walked away from the multitudes and told people to be quiet about what He had done. He never personally authored a single word, except for once when He wrote something in the sand.

'My thoughts are not your thoughts, neither are your ways my ways, declares the LORD.' (Isa. 55:8) Jesus had the Seventy, He called the Twelve, and He focused on the Three (Peter, James, and John). In their Gospel ministry they continued the leadership model implemented by Christ. Peter, along with Barnabas, helped to define, develop, and deploy a future leader named Saul of Tarsus, who was renamed Paul. Eventually, Paul had his own leadership team that was large, skilled, and effective. Not content with that, when the time came for him to leave this world, he prepared another new leader to carry his ministry forward. His name was Timothy, and with these inspired words Paul charged him to continue defining, developing and deploying leaders after the model of Christ: 'You then, my child, be strengthened by the grace that is in Christ Jesus, and what you have heard from me in the presence of many witnesses entrust to faithful men who will be able to teach others also.' (2 Tim. 2:1-2)

All of these things that were recorded in the New Testament had Old Testament precedents, of course. Prior to the sending of Christ into the world, this same paradigm of defining, developing, and deploying leaders was practiced throughout the history of Israel. Moses did it with leaders like the Hebrew elders and his successor Joshua. David had his three mighty men and his thirty men of renown. Elijah had Elisha and his school of prophets.

The model Christ revealed in His incarnation was rooted in the Old Testament, and fully bloomed in the New Testament.

Its effectiveness as a strategy was affirmed even by its frustrated adversaries, and it needs to be re-established in the church today. The opportunity is before us, and I would love to hear an adversary again say, 'These men who have turned the world upside down have come here also' (Acts 17:6). But if we desire to hear those kinds of things said about the church today, we must prioritize defining, developing, and deploying leaders. 'These men' who were world-shapers did not just appear; they were intentionally raised up as a part of a biblical process.

> Almost two thousand years ago Jesus initiated the model of 3D Leadership – He *defined, developed*, and *deployed* leaders who in turn repeated the same model, and in less than a generation the known world was turned upside down.

The model at work in church history

Christ's incarnational model of leadership not only transformed the first century world, but we see God using it providentially throughout church history. Martin Luther was raised up to initiate the Reformation. Then Luther developed leaders such as Ulrich Zwingli, Philipp Melanchthon, and hundreds of others who made the Reformation a roaring stream of Gospel truth that revitalized the church and spread throughout the world. John Calvin's devotion to producing leaders for world evangelism was extraordinary: he developed thirteen hundred missionaries just for France alone, and even sent a team of trained leaders to take the Gospel to what is today Rio de Janeiro, Brazil. John Knox multiplied his leadership with his 'black-robed militia' – Gospel preachers in Geneva gowns whom he had trained to live out his prayer of 'Give me Scotland, or I die.'

As leaders multiplied from the Reformation just in time for the Age of Discovery, the revival jumped the Atlantic and spilled into North America. It laid the groundwork for the culture of the thirteen colonies and led to the Great Awakening in eighteenth-century America and England. That remarkable move of God prepared Americans for independence and laid a spiritual foundation for American culture and government. It also blessed

England by sparing it from the humanism that smothered France in the French Revolution, and by spurring a golden age of British evangelism.

As leaders multiplied leaders, the Christian church in England and America spawned a massive missionary movement that eventually covered most of the globe and is even now transforming Africa, South America, and Asia.

That's why the leaders of today's church must return to the Christ-given model of leadership – leaders identifying leaders, molding them, and multiplying them. It's God's strategy that was modeled by Christ, implanted in the Old Testament, implemented by the Apostles, reclaimed by the Reformation, and spread worldwide by the Great Awakening. It will produce fruit unlike anything we can copy from the world. So as we begin anew, let us join together in this prayer: 'Lord, please launch a movement of grace for the kingdom of God in our day today. Father! Please! Do it again, and do it through us!'

What do successful multiplication leaders look like? Thankfully, again, the Scriptures are not silent. Jesus has taught us what these leaders should be, so let's put 'first things first'. Before we can develop and deploy such world-shaking leaders, we need to understand what they are according to the Word.

The Definition of a Biblical Leader

Matthew 28:16-20 says:

> Now the eleven disciples went to Galilee, to the mountain to which Jesus had directed them. And when they saw Him they worshiped Him, but some doubted. And Jesus came and said to them, 'All authority in heaven and on earth has been given to me. Go therefore and make disciples of all nations, baptizing them in the name of the Father and of the Son and of the Holy Spirit, teaching them to observe all that I have commanded you. And behold, I am with you always, to the end of the age.'

In those words, and in the effect they had on His disciples, Jesus exemplified what made Him such a great and influential leader. They reflect and illustrate the content of a short definition of leadership that I have found helpful: *A leader influences others to effectively achieve a defined mission together.* Let's take some time to 'unpack' that definition, focusing especially on the concepts represented by the three words *influence*, *effectively*, and *together*.

The influence of a good leader

The first key word in that definition is *influence*. Jesus, of course, was the most influential person who ever lived on this planet. And in His earthly ministry He lived out every one of the following points, which describe the kind of leader who will truly be a 'person of influence'. Each one contains a leadership skill, followed by how God uses that skill and what He wants to achieve in the people being influenced by the leader.

First, an influential leader is a *model* who *embodies* for the purpose of *imitation*. If a leader doesn't model integrity, then he or she may be dismissed as a hypocrite, no matter how good a teacher he or she may be. There's much truth in the old adage, 'Make sure your walk matches your talk.' Modeling is a major key to having the opportunity to influence others, and especially other leaders.

In Acts 1:1, Luke refers to his Gospel by saying: 'In the first book, O Theophilus, I have dealt with all that Jesus began to do and teach.' Notice the wording there about Christ – He began to *do* (modeling) and *teach* (mentoring). It's interesting that Luke puts those two things in that order, because many times modeling precedes mentoring. For instance, as a result of seeing Jesus pray, His disciples asked Him, 'Lord, teach us to pray.' (Luke 11:1)

Effective disciple-making in general, and leadership training in particular, require consistent modeling to open the door to the necessary relationships, and to solidify them. 'Doing' in the life of a leader is the gateway to 'teaching' in the lives of future leaders. Consider this illustration: Although babies have the capacity to communicate, they don't come out with a particular language programmed into their DNA. Yet within a few years, they learn to speak their native tongue. They're taught a language entirely by a non-professional (usually their mother), who doesn't have any kind of degree or even training in language education.

How is that possible? First, the baby is nurtured and encouraged by a mother's persevering love. Additionally, all humans are born imitators. Paul reflects this in 1 Corinthians 4:15-16: 'I became your father in Christ Jesus through the Gospel. I urge you, then, be imitators of me.' According to some estimates, 80 percent of what is learned comes through imitation and 20 percent by instruction. The 20 per cent is crucial because it establishes what ought to be imitated and how to conserve it, but most of what we learn is acquired by observing others. Therefore, being a model with integrity of character must be a priority for any leader.

> A leader influences others to effectively achieve a defined mission together.

Secondly, an influential leader is a *mentor* who *educates* for the purpose of *instruction*. No matter how much people might admire a leader's example, they still cannot do the right thing until they know the right thing. Therefore, leaders must have the skills of a *mentor* and *educator*. For example, the book of Acts says that the evangelist Apollos was inspired and passionate for the Lord's work, but had inaccurate knowledge that was limiting his ministry. Two leaders who had been developed by Paul – Aquila and Priscilla – 'took him aside and explained to him the way of God more accurately' (Acts 18:26). They influenced him to be a better man and minister by their mentoring and instruction.

Thirdly, an influential leader is a *motivator* who *empowers* for the purpose of *inspiration*. In the deadly trench warfare of World War I, Colonel Douglas MacArthur – who later, as General MacArthur, would drive Imperial Japanese forces across the Pacific in World War II – was ordered to cross 'no-man's land' and assault a German-fortified position. All previous efforts to take the post had failed. MacArthur knew that success – and survival – depended on his leadership. He assigned his second-in-command, an army major, the task of leading the charge against the left flank of the enemy position.

'Sir, I place you on the left side,' MacArthur explained. 'I will lead from the center.'

Then, having already been a model and mentor to this young leader, MacArthur moved into the role of motivator.

'I know that you are capable of leading the men on to victory,' he told the major. Then MacArthur pointed to a medal awarded for courage that was pinned on his own uniform. 'When this battle is over,' he said, 'I'll see to it that you get one of these.'

MacArthur turned and walked away, but then spun around and strode back to the young officer. He removed his medal and pinned it on the surprised major.

'I know what kind of man you are,' MacArthur told him. 'I'm not going to wait for the end of this battle to give you this medal. Here, I'll give you mine now. I'll see you at the top.'

What do you think happened? The young major bravely took the enemy position – largely because MacArthur had influenced him through embodiment, education, and empowerment.

Fourthly, an influential leader is a *manager* who *equips* for the purpose of *implementation*. As a manager, the leader provides resources needed for people to do what they have been called to do. Nothing is more frustrating than to be given a job without being equipped to do the work. An effective leader will manage the ultimate delivery of the resources and equipment necessary to complete the mission.

Finally, an influential leader is a *minister* who *evaluates* for the purpose of *improvement*. Good leaders love those they lead, enough to make time for both encouragement and learning when a task has been accomplished. It's wrong-headed and wrong-hearted for leaders to move on to the next task without promoting celebration of a completed effort and constructive criticism for improvement in the lives of those who have served. To press on without taking the time to reflect can be demoralizing and counterproductive. But good Christian leaders stop to express thanks to God and His servants for the good things that have happened, and to lovingly encourage growth for what could have been done better.

The effectiveness of a good leader

'A leader influences others to effectively achieve a defined mission together.' The second key word in that definition is *effectively*. I'd like to make a distinction between 'effectiveness' and 'efficiency' which is a favorite term in Corporate America. Efficiency is an important part of true effectiveness in Christian leadership, but it is not the whole picture. Efficiency is useless if you don't pursue excellence in your work. And just because you get a lot done doesn't mean you are necessarily making the best use of your time. And all of that is pointless if it is not done with good motives. So effective leaders are those who *do the right things in the right way at the right time for the right reasons.* Let's take a closer look at these four principles:

1. The principle of *efficiency*: doing the right things.

2. The principle of *excellence*: doing the right things in the right way.

3. The principle of *economy*: doing the right things in the right way at the right time.

4. The principle of *exaltation*: doing the right things in the right way at the right time for the right reasons.

The first principle is that of *efficiency*: a commitment to doing the *right things.* In today's society, efficiency is often thought of in terms of multitasking – but doing the right thing is more important than doing many things. Consider this modified example from the book *First Things First:*[1]

> A professor set a large glass cylinder in front of his class. In it were several large rocks, with two others sitting nearby on the professor's desk.
>
> 'Is the jar full?' he asked the class. Most students agreed that the jar was full. The professor then shook it, causing the rocks to settle and making room for one more rock, which he placed inside it.
>
> 'Is the jar full now?' he asked.
>
> 'Yes,' the students concluded.
>
> The professor then produced a container of sand from beneath the desk and poured some of it into the cylinder. The sand settled into the spaces between the rocks.
>
> 'Is the jar full now?' he asked.

1. Stephen R. Covey, A. Roger Merrill, and Rebecca R. Merrill, *First Things First: To Live, to Love, to Learn, to Leave a Legacy* (New York: Simon & Schuster, 1994), pp. 88-94.

'No,' said most of the class members, catching on. Sure enough, the professor next poured some water into the jar, and it was finally truly filled.

'So what lessons did you learn?' he asked. One student suggested that there's always room to squeeze in a little more.

'True,' agreed the professor. 'You can usually squeeze a little more activity into your life and work – but that's not the main lesson.' The students looked puzzled.

'The main point,' the professor concluded, 'is that big rocks must go in first. To be truly effective, you must identify the big rocks in your life and place them as a priority in your schedule.'

So what are the 'big rocks' in your life, the ones that must be given first place in your calendar? For Christian leaders the big rocks are the biblically-revealed responsibilities and relationships that are crucial to effective living for the glory of God. They cannot be squeezed into life as an afterthought. Space must be allocated for them as a priority.

For example, good Christian leaders realize that daily time with the Lord in prayer and the Word is one of the big rocks. So is worship on the Lord's Day. Time with one's spouse is a big rock. The nurturing of the parent-child relationship is also. In other words, God's priorities – as taught in His Word – are the big rocks that we must give first place to in our life calendars. This is the principle of effectiveness – making and keeping a commitment to do the right things. So take out your day timer and put in the 'big rocks' first.

> Effective leaders are those who do the right things in the right way at the right time for the right reasons.

The second principle of effective leadership is a commitment to *excellence:* doing the right things *in the right way.* When we stand before our Savior, what do we want to hear Him say? 'Well done, good and faithful servant,' right? That should be our desire, according to Matthew 25:21. Notice that the first word in that statement is '*well*' – the principle of excellence. That's more than just '*done*,' more than merely being acceptable or mediocre. '*Well* done' is what we want to hear the Lord say to us. Few of us will ever be the best at anything, but all of us can do our best. That's what we do when we do the right things in the right way as an offering of praise to our glorious Savior.

My parents – and yours, too, probably – used to say, 'Son, if it's worth doing, it's worth doing right.' That's the principle of excellence. The right thing (efficiency) is worth doing, and it's worth doing in the right way (excellence).

Next is the principle of *economy*: doing the right thing in the right way *at the right time* – or doing more than one thing at a time when it's appropriate. (Today it's often called 'multitasking'.)

When I was a child, my father, who was in baseball, arranged for me to be excused from school for two weeks to join him on a road trip. It was exciting to be able to spend time with him and watch him at work. When I had children of my own, this was one way that I wanted to imitate my father. So I usually tried to take one of my children with me when I spoke at a conference, visited someone in the hospital, or went on a short-term missions trip. This allowed me to fulfill my calling as a pastor/teacher while also spending meaningful time with my children, and it was one of the blessings of the principle of efficiency thoughtfully applied.

I've also tried to apply this principle by taking others with me on hospital calls, mission trips, and various other ministry opportunities. I usually invite members of our church leadership team to join me, so that not only am I fulfilling my pastoral ministry, I'm also including others – which blesses and assists me in ministry while honing their leadership skills as we debrief about the experience, considering the Lord's blessings and the lessons learned.

The concluding principle of *exaltation* is simply doing everything *for the right reasons*. The first and foremost reason is 'to glorify God and enjoy Him forever' (Westminster Catechism question and answer 1). The second reason is for the edification, or the building up, of others. For instance, Ephesians 4:29 says that we are to communicate with other believers not in order to 'vent' or 'get something off my chest,' which is a self-directed motive, but instead to 'give grace to those who hear.' Likewise, 1 Thessalonians

5:11 says we should 'encourage one another and build one another up.' So we should do what we do to exalt God, and also to lift up others.

This twofold principle of exaltation is reflected in the Great Commandment: 'Love the Lord your God with all your heart and with all your soul and with all your mind ... [and] love your neighbor as yourself' (Matt. 22:37-39). We see this principle modeled by the Apostles John and Paul. John 'rejoiced greatly to find some of your children walking in the truth' (2 John 1:4), and Paul's zeal to glorify the Lord was inseparably connected with a concern for the well-being of others (Rom. 8:21; 2 Cor. 4:15; Phil. 1:11).

One final thought on effectiveness. As Christians, and especially as Christian leaders, we should prefer the concept of 'spending' time over 'managing' it. We never want to squander the precious resource of time, but spending it means focusing on investing it joyfully, wisely, and unselfishly – rather than always trying to 'beat the clock'. We are born into this world with a finite number of sunrises and sunsets. While many resources are renewable, our days are not. They don't need to be managed – we need to be managed. The Scripture calls us to 'redeem the time'.

Once we 'spend' a day or even an hour or a moment, we do not get it back. So spend them efficiently with a commitment to excellence and an eye on economy, for the purpose of exalting God and encouraging others. We don't usually fail because we can't do more than one thing at a time; we fail because too often we don't do the right thing in the right way at the right time for the right reasons.

The teamwork of a good leader

'A leader influences others to effectively achieve a defined mission *together.*' When a Christian servant leader does that, people will bond together as a team. But how does a team achieve success, and how does it complete its mission with unity? Again, the answer lies in the biblical model of leadership, summarized in three powerful team-building dynamics.

The first key to a unified, motivated team is *acceptance of the team leader.* A title does not a leader make. It's only when people follow that a leader can truly lead. So one of the responsibilities of a leader is to make sure that everyone is on the right team. If some team members don't accept their leader, they should be encouraged to seek another team, no matter how valuable they may appear to be. Diversity brings strength, but only with unity – and team unity begins with acceptance of the team leader. The leader must be supported, embraced, encouraged, and followed by the team.

A second factor in bringing people together is *acceptance of the team's defined mission*. Without a mutual commitment to a common objective, a team cannot function. This means that team members should put aside personal agendas and embrace the mission along with the leader.

Third, it's also crucial for team members to have acceptance for one another. To successfully complete the mission, they should appreciate each other and each other's responsibilities. This means that all team members should look for opportunities to support and encourage each other, in both good times and bad.

A good leader will consistently and unrelentingly teach and promote these team dynamics, which we see illustrated well in the Old Testament book of Nehemiah.

The Lord gave Nehemiah, as the leader of His people, the vitally important mission of rebuilding the wrecked wall of Jerusalem. The people accepted his leadership. They accepted the mission. They accepted one another. And they achieved success. Their humble, determined attitude honored the Lord and made them an effective team. When they unified in accepting Nehemiah as their leader, collectively embracing the mission and accepting one another as team members, they were empowered – and they rebuilt the wall of Jerusalem as God intended. The Word of God records the result: 'the people had a mind to work' (Neh. 4:6), and they completed their massive project in record time (Neh. 6:15).

Most teams consist of disconnected people doing their particular job and hoping it works out. I compare them to golf teams. On a golf team each golfer plays his own game, and then everyone adds up all of their scores at the end. But good teams are more like those in football: everyone has a responsibility, but all are playing the same game and attempting to score by crossing the same goal line. Not only do they have their personal assignment but they also have a responsibility to assist one another. The team scores. The team wins. The team crosses the goal line – together. If a great catch was made in the end zone, the quarterback threw it, the offensive line protected the quarterback, other receivers distracted the defense, and the result is that the team scores – not just the person who caught the ball. So it can be for us today. Imagine what would happen to our culture – to our world – if it could be said of the contemporary American church that we 'had a mind' to work together.

Not only do good leaders influence others to effectively achieve a defined mission together, but they also have some absolutely non-negotiable personal qualities that are required for long-term effective leadership. Christian leadership is a privilege, not a right, and is dependent on one's progress in the Gospel. It does not come about simply because we have been converted to faith in Christ, but because we have grown in Christ. We'll learn more about what that Gospel progress looks like in the next chapter.

Questions for Thought and Discussion

1) What does Mark 10:42-45 tell us about the 'incarnational model' of Christ's leadership? How can you apply it to your life and leadership?

2) Who are some leaders in the history of the church that you admire, and what made them good leaders?

3) Charles Spurgeon once issued this warning: 'Beware that you don't unsay with your life what you've said with your tongue.' Have you seen that happen, and how could it have been avoided?

4) How could you make better use of your time in ministry? Could you take someone along with you when you are doing it?

5) Has God used you to 'influence others to effectively achieve a defined mission together'? Take some time to pray that He will do so in the days to come.

Chapter 3

The Qualifications of a Christian Leader

THE foundational texts for leadership in the church are contained in two familiar passages in Scripture. They are easy to find and are relatively easy to understand. Unfortunately they are also too often ignored. With saddening frequency, Christian congregations and church authorities choose leaders based on their occupations, personalities, or professional achievements, rather than the biblical qualifications for leadership. The result is that church congregations remain spiritually immature. False doctrine is taught. Biblical truth is neglected. Pastors are dismissed. Churches split apart. Members are distracted, disgruntled, or disheartened. The work of the church grows cold and the opportunity to model and mentor leaders in the church for deployment into the world is squandered.

Biblical truth transforms, but it must be known and applied. So what are the key texts on the required marks of a Christian leader? They are found in 1 Timothy 3 and Titus 1:

> The saying is trustworthy: If anyone aspires to the office of overseer, he desires a noble task. Therefore an overseer must be above reproach, the husband of one wife, sober-minded, self-controlled, respectable, hospitable, able to teach, not a drunkard, not violent but gentle, not quarrelsome, not a lover of money. He must manage his own household well, with all dignity keeping his children submissive, for if someone does not know how to manage his own household, how will he care for God's church? He must not be a recent convert, or he may become puffed up with conceit and fall into the condemnation of the devil. Moreover, he must be well

thought of by outsiders, so that he may not fall into disgrace, into a snare of the devil. (1 Tim. 3:1-7)

> This is why I left you in Crete, so that you might put what remained into order, and appoint elders in every town as I directed you – if anyone is above reproach, the husband of one wife, and his children are believers and not open to the charge of debauchery or insubordination. For an overseer, as God's steward, must be above reproach. He must not be arrogant or quick-tempered or a drunkard or violent or greedy for gain, but hospitable, a lover of good, self-controlled, upright, holy, and disciplined. He must hold firm to the trustworthy word as taught, so that he may be able to give instruction in sound doctrine and also to rebuke those who contradict it. (Titus 1:5-9)

The content of these passages can be summarized by saying that there are two basic qualifications for a leader in God's church: *A Divine calling and a Godly character*. These set the definition of Christian leadership apart from the world's, and there is no true Christian leadership without them. Recovering them will position the church to produce world-changing leaders who are able to impact every sphere of society. But if they continue to be ignored and neglected, the deployment of impact leaders for the world will remain nothing more than a thing of the past.

A Divine Calling

The first requirement for leadership in God's church is the existence of a Divine 'call'. God Himself decides whom He wants as leaders in His Church, and He communicates that by His Holy Spirit to the individual, and also to the whole body. Let's learn more about this Divine call from the Scripture.

The call is both internal and external

The *internal* call is given by the Holy Spirit to motivate someone who has the spiritual gifts needed for a particular leadership role. That call is described in 1 Timothy 3:1: 'If anyone *aspires* to the office of overseer, he *desires* a noble task.' Note the words *aspires* and *desires*. God moves in the hearts of potential leaders to equip them with a passion to lead and a selfless motivation for becoming a leader. The word *selfless* is crucial. The internal call is not the drive of an inflated ego or the maneuvering of a manipulator to control others or gain power. As we will discuss further in the next section, the church is in need of leaders who desire the work of a leader not simply the position or title of a leader.

But even though the motive should not be a selfish one, a desire still must be present for someone to be a true Christian leader. 1 Peter 5:1-3 says:

> I exhort the elders among you, as a fellow elder and a witness of the sufferings of Christ, as well as a partaker in the glory that is going to be revealed: shepherd the flock of God that is among you, exercising oversight, *not under compulsion*, but willingly, as God would have you; not for shameful gain, *but eagerly*; not domineering over those in your charge, but being examples to the flock. [author's italics]

We should not become leaders in the church merely out of a sense of duty or a feeling of guilt. We should not do it because 'there's no one else available,' 'no one else who can do it as well as me,' and certainly not because we are in need of an income. Peter says that leaders should serve 'eagerly' – that is the internal call Paul is describing in 1 Timothy 3:1.

The *external* call is communicated by the Holy Spirit to others in the church. Those who sense an internal call should submit themselves to the existing leadership of the church, and to the body as well, for verification and affirmation. Paul's instructions about leadership qualifications are given to Timothy and Titus, who had already been ordained by other elders (1 Tim. 4:14), and had also been given authority to appoint other leaders (Titus 1:6). 1 Timothy 3:10 speaks of leaders being 'tested first' before being put into positions of leadership. And Romans 10:15 says: 'How are they to preach unless they are sent?' Leaders must have the affirmation of those who have mentored and observed them. Those who will serve with them in leadership and those they would lead must be able to affirm the internal call with an external call.

So a leader should be both called and affirmed – internally called by the Holy Spirit and externally affirmed by Spirit-led church leaders and members. It is a humbling experience to submit to the evaluation of others in the church, but it is also liberating and empowering. Jesus Christ, who humbled Himself to come

into this world, commands us to submit and exercise humility –
and that includes aspiring leaders. 'Humble yourselves, therefore,
under the mighty hand of God so that at the proper time He may
exalt you.' (1 Pet. 5:6)

> God Himself decides who He wants as leaders in His Church,
> and He communicates that by His Holy Spirit to the individual,
> and also to the whole body.

The call is to a work more than a position

'Why do you want to become an elder in the church?' a man was
once asked.

'Well, I'd like to be able to change the way things are done
around here,' he answered.

'Do you have a desire in your heart to do ministries like teaching
the Word, counseling people about their problems, visiting the
sick, or practicing church discipline?'

'No, not really,' he said. 'I just want to have a say.'

That man was not qualified to serve as a leader in God's church,
because *leaders are to be position-bearers, not position-wearers*.
What's the difference? For the answer, examine 1 Timothy 3:1 carefully: 'If anyone aspires to the office of overseer, he desires *a noble
task*.'

That text teaches that leadership is a *task* – a noble task indeed,
but still a *task*. In other words, leadership is hard work. It is a call
to commitment that requires physical, mental, emotional, and
spiritual exercise and sacrifice. Christian leaders must be mature,
disciplined, and respected because the pressures of leadership
multiply the challenges of life. For instance, a leader must sometimes endure sustained or frequent attacks by sideline critics and
skeptics, and still remain loving and focused. The leader also
immediately goes into the crosshairs of Satan, who wants to scatter
the sheep by striking down the shepherd. Leadership is a call of love
and passion, but it is also hard work from a mature faith rooted in
the sufficiency of Christ. It requires growing in grace, maturing in
leadership, and walking confidently and carefully in Christ.

Life is messy, and a leader is required to sacrificially wade into that messiness with the love and truth of Jesus Christ. That is why a Christian leader must aspire to be a position-bearer, not a position-wearer. He or she doesn't accept a call to leadership in order to acquire a title, to expand a résumé, or to build a future obituary. Instead, genuine leaders exercise leadership to exalt the Lord and shepherd their families and the church while thoughtfully committing to influence the world for Christ and reproduce leaders who will shake the world.

Furthermore, the work of leadership is also an act of worship. We should embrace that work with the same passion we are to bring to the act of corporate worship. That's why Paul urged Timothy to 'fulfill your ministry' (2 Tim. 4:5). The call to leadership is not a call to fulfill yourself but to fulfill the ministry. Paul's objective was not self-fulfillment, but self-sacrifice for ministry fulfillment. This is why he said, just prior to his death: 'I am already being poured out as a drink offering.' (2 Tim. 4:6) That was not a statement of self-congratulation, but a declaration of thanksgiving to his God who had called him to spiritual life and leadership. Burnt offerings have ashes left over at the end, but drink offerings have nothing left. Paul had fulfilled his ministry by emptying himself to love and lead for Christ.

That leads us to the second basic qualification for true Christian leadership.

A Godly Character

Godliness is more important than giftedness. Never is that saying more true than when it comes to leadership, and we need to be reminded of it because of the temptation to get it backwards.

Chapter 3 of 1 Timothy lists twenty-seven qualifications and Titus 1 has seventeen of them, and *all but one or two* are clearly issues of character rather than giftedness. They could possibly *all* be about character, because 'able to teach' could also be translated as 'teachable' and 'children who believe' might simply be a way of re-stating 'manages his household well'. It is significant to note that when Paul wrote his longest explanations about the qualifications for leadership, he wasn't concerned much, if at all, about how talented the leader was, or even how many people wanted to follow him. What was on his mind more than anything was the personal godliness of the candidate.

While giftedness is important, a gifted leader who lacks godliness can lead others to destruction, and even bring destruction upon himself. Personal godliness is simply not optional: 'An overseer *must be* above reproach.' (1 Tim. 3:2) When God develops the heart of a leader, there is evidence of the grace that produces godliness (Titus 2:11-14). A leader's character is forged from a pattern of loving submission to the One who possesses him, his life, and his leadership.

> Life is messy, and a leader is required to sacrificially wade into that messiness with the love and truth of Jesus Christ.

A grace-driven, disciplined lifestyle

In order to have the Godly character required, leaders must display a discernible pattern of discipline. For example, 1 Timothy 3 makes clear that they must be practicing it in their own personal choices: 'An overseer must be above reproach, the husband of one wife, sober-minded, self-controlled, respectable, hospitable, able to teach.' (v. 2) And their families should display a faithful, God-centered environment: 'He must manage his own household well, with all dignity, keeping his children submissive, for if someone does not know how to manage his own household, how will he care for God's church?' (vv. 4-5) Then according to verse 6, a leader should not be a 'novice' or a 'recent convert,' which means they have practiced the pattern of personal discipline long enough to be considered spiritually mature. Finally, verse 7 reveals that they should be 'well thought of by outsiders'.

Biblical leaders are disciplined and mature believers who effectively lead their homes, enjoy the affirmation of their spiritual maturity by the congregation, and have a respected witness in the surrounding secular community. Think about it in reverse order: leaders can't have a positive effect on the surrounding community without having the respect of their congregation. And they can't be effective in the church without managing their families well.

And all of this requires the ongoing vitality of personal spiritual health and growth.

Here is an illustration that I remember from my first pastorate, which was in the Miami area. One evening I attended a meeting at a spectacular hotel in Miami Beach. It had a magnificent fountain in the lobby. Water rose from a reservoir and flowed into a small laver. From there, the water overflowed into another laver, then into another – and finally it flowed into a basin from which it was recycled. I've often thought of that fountain as a wonderful analogy of the work of grace in the life of a believer. The grace of Jesus Christ is propelled by the Holy Spirit (as He illuminates God's Word) into the believer's personal life; then – like the water flowing through the fountain's lavers – it overflows into the believer's family, then into the church, and finally into the community.

You may have heard this said about priorities: Put God first, then family, church, work, community, and everything else. That's a very common idea, but is it biblical? Scripture certainly does emphasize putting God and others first before self, but I believe Scripture reveals a much more foundational approach to lifestyle prioritizing. God is not at the top of our priority list, He is our list. Each item on our list should be all about Him.

Our Lord does not simply call us to put Him first in life, but for Him to be our life. This passion for the pre-eminence of Christ caused the Apostle Paul to write: 'For to me to live is Christ' (Phil. 1:21) and 'Christ, who is your life' (Col. 3:4). We're not commanded to love God with most of our heart, mind, and soul but with all of our heart, mind and soul. Believers' lives should be Christ-centered and Christ-consumed. As the lordship of Christ transforms us, the priorities of life will, of necessity, be established by Him as our Lord. Personal formation, family formation, church participation, and community impact will be the result. True biblical leaders show the way with lives framed by Christ-given priorities as they live their lives fully and completely given to Him.

Three traps to avoid

Knowing that biblical leadership is a privilege rather than an entitlement, and that Satan especially targets leaders, we must be careful to avoid his traps. A Christian leader has been saved by grace like any other believer and is undergoing the progressive refining that every Christian experiences. Yet the privilege of Christian leadership can be forfeited if a leader engages in deliberate or scandalous behavior and is no longer above reproach.

Three problems that have entrapped countless Christian leaders are *indolence, immorality,* and *insubordination.* Upon these dangerous rocks many leaders have shipwrecked not only their leadership, but also their own relationship with Christ, their families, and the ministries they've led. The world's leaders may have one or more of these sins in their lives, and may even celebrate them, but they have absolutely no place in the lives of Christian leaders.

Indolence is habitual laziness, which is a crime against followers who are dependent on their leaders in many ways and deserve our best efforts. Certainly our work must be measured and planned to include rest and recreation, but a Christian leader should never be vulnerable to the accusation of laziness. The Bible clearly teaches that an undisciplined, unmotivated lifestyle does not glorify God and is harmful to others. For example, Proverbs 18:9 says, 'Whoever is slack in his work is a brother to him who destroys', and in 2 Thessalonians 3:6 we are commanded to 'keep away from any brother who is walking in idleness.'

In contrast, the lifestyle of a genuine Christian leader is marked by industriousness. Scripture reveals that Jesus was never hurried or frenzied. He was always going 'straightway' or 'immediately' to the next Divine appointment. His lifestyle was energetic but focused, and He properly sustained His leadership activity with appropriate periods of physical and spiritual renewal and rest. Leaders who emulate their Savior will work hard to be prepared for the coming of a crisis and will not be found AWOL (Absent Without Leave) when the moment of need arrives.

A Christian leader has been saved by grace like any other believer and is undergoing the progressive refining that every Christian experiences. Yet the privilege of Christian leadership can be forfeited if a leader engages in deliberate or scandalous behavior and is no longer above reproach.

Immorality is probably the most prevalent sin destroying Christian leaders today – especially sexual immorality. Most of us could list numerous leaders whose lives, families, and ministries have been wrecked or damaged by this sin.

Can a leader who falls to adultery or fornication be restored and reconciled in the home and in the church? Yes – sexual immorality is not the unforgivable sin. But it *is* extremely destructive to the element of trust that is so essential to leadership, and full restoration to authority will, of necessity, require much supervised time and effort.

God's advice on this issue is powerfully simple and effective: *flee temptation*. Satan's assault is incessant. Contemporary American culture is a hypersexualized society that flaunts sexual impropriety, promiscuity, and perversion. We are to flee temptation. Do not try to resist it – *flee it*.

> Blessed is the man who remains steadfast under trial, for when he has stood the test he will receive the crown of life, which God has promised to those who love Him. Let no one say when he is tempted, 'I am being tempted by God,' for God cannot be tempted with evil, and He Himself tempts no one. But each person is tempted when he is lured and enticed by his own desire. Then desire when it has conceived gives birth to sin, and sin when it is fully grown brings forth death. (James 1:12-15)

How do you flee temptation? In most cases it's relatively simple: avoid putting yourself in harm's way. Run from any and all occasions where you might be tempted. Christian leaders should make a covenant with the Lord concerning sexual purity before marriage and sexual faithfulness within marriage. This should include a commitment to guard your eyes, your thoughts, and your conversation, as well as your actions. Honor God's ordinance of marriage by abstaining from all sinful sexual activity before and during marriage, and regularly enjoying God-created sexual love within marriage (1 Cor. 7:1-5).

A practical defensive weapon against Satan's attacks in this age is an accountability partner or group. For over thirty years I have been blessed by the redemptive relationships in such a group. It is my 'band of brothers'. Each of us has made a vow that if one of us appears to falter in the area of sexual immorality, the others will hold him accountable and help restore him back into a walk with the Lord, the church, and most of all his family and marriage. At the same time, we have agreed collectively that if any one of us succumbs to immorality by violating our marriage covenant, he must leave the pastoral ministry. For us, the door to leadership and ministry swings open one way and only one time. We did not make this agreement because we presume to possess exceptional character – quite the opposite actually. We hold each other accountable because we fully understand our inherent sinfulness and our ever-present weaknesses. Therefore, if or when we are tempted to engage in any kind of unfaithfulness, we must admit to ourselves: This will bring shame on the Lord's name and it will cost me my ministry. Is it worth it? By establishing a structure of accountability, we are striving to flee temptation before it even occurs. We call all of our voluntary accountabilities 'obstacles to sin' and 'stepping stones to obedience'.

Insubordination is another failure that can disqualify someone from Christian leadership. The Bible is powerfully frank on this subject: it demands that all believers and all churches embrace the doctrine of submission. If a leader cannot submit to others, he is unprepared to lead anyone else. Ephesians 5:21 says that all believers should be 'submitting to one another out of reverence for Christ', and Hebrews 13:17 says: 'Obey your leaders and submit to them.' Church members must submit to leaders, and leaders must submit to those in authority over them.

If you cannot submit, you should not expect others to submit to you. In fact, leaders must intentionally and openly exhibit a lifestyle of submission to those in authority over them. The privilege of leadership does not elevate the leader above submission; instead, it calls the leader to be a model of it. There is no such thing as an independent Christian or an independent leader. Submitting to one another is a crucial way in which our dependence on the Lord is manifested and demonstrated. So if a leader displays habitual insubordination, he is biblically unqualified for leadership.

Those who are qualified to be Christian leaders according to Scripture, as we have learned, are those who have a Divine call and Godly character. Those are the bottom line, lowest-common-denominator requirements in the Bible's definition of Christian leadership. But before we end our discussion of how to define it biblically, we want to learn more about how a leader can go beyond mere acceptability and ascend to exceptionality. In the next chapter, we'll learn what it takes for someone to be a truly great leader, by the grace and power of God.

Questions for Thought and Discussion

1) What are some reasons why people who want to be church leaders must have the right motives? What are some wrong motives they can have?

2) What are some aspects of being a church leader that can be difficult, and how could each of them end up being a blessing from God?

3) What is the difference between being qualified for church leadership (which some people are) and being perfect (which no one is)? What indications do you see in 1 Timothy 3 and Titus 1 that Paul is talking about the former rather than the latter?

4) What are some other ways Satan tries to make people disqualified for leadership, besides the three mentioned in the chapter? How can you avoid those traps?

5) Evaluate your life based on the leadership qualifications in 1 Timothy 3 and Titus 1, and identify at least three needed areas of growth. Take some time to pray about them, either by yourself or with others.

Chapter 4

What Makes a Leader Great?

DURING his presidency, Ronald Reagan was very contro-versial. Today we often hear positive things from both sides of the aisle about our fortieth president's political wisdom and personal fortitude. But if you're old enough to have lived during Ronald Reagan's two-term presidency, you probably remember how unpopular he was in some circles, especially for his denouncements of communism.

When Reagan took office, the United States was at the low point of a period of appeasement with the Soviet Union. It was a well-intentioned but obviously naïve approach – pretending that the Soviets really didn't want to take over the world and install totalitarian communism everywhere, while we basically begged them to play nice. But the policy of appeasement didn't work. Instead of respecting the autonomy of other nations and granting freedom to the Eastern European nations they already suppressed, the Soviet leadership promoted the violent communist takeover of one nation after another: Afghanistan, Angola, Mozambique, Nicaragua, Grenada.

As the new president of the United States, Ronald Reagan repeatedly offered to negotiate with the Soviets, but only from a position of American strength. His policy was 'Trust and Verify'. He believed that the Russian leaders were morally bankrupt and therefore could not be trusted without verification of what they said. He also believed that communism would implode if America stood firm for freedom. He built up the U.S. military from a state of

57

decline, called for liberty for all people oppressed by communism, and courageously called on the Soviet leadership to renounce what he called their 'evil empire'. He clearly stated his position to a 1983 convention of the National Association of Evangelicals:

> Yes, let us pray for the salvation of all of those who live in that totalitarian darkness – pray they will discover the joy of knowing God. But until they do, let us be aware that while they preach the supremacy of the state, declare its omnipotence over individual man, and predict its eventual domination of all peoples on the Earth, they are the focus of evil in the modern world.[1]

Many people were really upset by Reagan's words. This affable, easygoing American leader became extremely controversial. Newspaper editors, television commentators, political opponents, foreign leaders, Hollywood celebrities, and others were harshly critical of him. They ridiculed his policy, his intelligence, his character, his age, and even his hair. But he proved them all wrong. Eventually the communist Soviet Union collapsed, unable to match Reagan's defense buildup, unable to disprove his 'evil empire' accusation, and unable to repress the desire for freedom from the millions within its sphere – including countless Christians. Led by Ronald Reagan, the United States won the Cold War.

Leadership works. Good leadership produces good results and bad leadership produces bad results. Jesus affirms this when He says: 'It is enough for the disciple to be like his teacher, and the servant like his master' (Matt. 10:25), and 'if the blind lead the blind, both will fall into a pit.' (Matt. 15:14) Since leadership works, to get great results we need to define, develop, and deploy great leaders.

Ronald Wilson Reagan was not a perfect man, of course, but in many ways he was a great leader. If you had told those of us who were growing up in the 1960s that the Berlin Wall would be torn down and communism would collapse in on itself, we would have dismissed you as at best naïve and possibly insane. Reagan saw what needed to happen, what could happen, and how it needed to happen, and he led the way.

---

1. *Tear Down This Wall: The Reagan Revolution – A National Review History*, compiled by the editors of *National Review* (New York: Continuum, 2004), p. 35.

The church today needs to understand what makes a great leader in God's eyes. By the power of the Holy Spirit, we can raise up leaders that will impact the world *even more* than Ronald Reagan did, because they will be winning spiritual battles and producing eternal outcomes, not just temporary political ones. But to do that we need to understand four maxims about leadership that arise from the Scriptures.

Great Leaders Know their Mission and are Unalterably Committed to Achieving It

How did Reagan do it? How did he remain unwavering under such a harsh and prolonged assault by his own countrymen, as well as foreign enemies? He knew his mission. He was steadfastly committed to achieving it, he refused to be paralyzed by fear, and with passion he communicated the mission and the strategy for its success.

We have been given an even better example of this in Jesus Christ, who was unalterably committed to achieving His mission. He came into this world to save sinners, defeat Satan, and win the victory for His church. He allowed nothing to deter Him. The dread of the cup of suffering that He would drink, the fearsome challenge of facing a horrible death, and even His 'descent into hell' and separation from the Father would not keep Him from achieving His mission.

That kind of focus and passion should consume leaders who are following Christ as their Lord and Savior. Great leadership requires an understanding of our mission and an unyielding commitment of faithfulness to it. Neither self-promotion, nor self-preservation, nor pride, nor fear, nor weariness should deter a leader from faithfully fulfilling the mission.

For Christian leaders, our marching orders are both simple and profound. First, we are called to personally 'seek first the kingdom of God and his righteousness, and all these things will be added to you' (Matt. 6:33). Second, we must continually reproduce ourselves by making disciples who have an unquenchable passion for the pre-eminence of Christ in all things (Col. 1:18). Finally, we execute our specific responsibilities as a Christian leader in the task, initiative, or organization that has been entrusted to us.

> *Leadership works.* Good leadership produces good results and bad leadership produces bad results.

Great Leaders Take Care of their People

Our Lord Jesus, again, is the ultimate example of this maxim. His loving concern for His people is demonstrated in so many ways in the Gospels and elsewhere in Scripture, but here are just a few examples.

In John 17, we read that on the night before Jesus' unjust trial, terrible scourging and crucifixion (not to mention the horrors of being separated from His father through bearing the penalty of sin) the chapter describes Him serving His disciples by praying for them. One of His primary requests in this long intercessory prayer is for the protection of His followers, which is consistent with His vigilant care for them throughout His earthly ministry. 'I do not ask that you take them out of the world,' He prays, 'but that you protect them from the evil one.' (John 17:15)

Who can forget these famous words from our Lord: 'I am the good shepherd ... I lay down my life for the sheep.' (John 10:14-15) He made use of a similar analogy during His leadership training of the disciples:

> What do you think? If a man has a hundred sheep, and one of them has gone astray, does he not leave the ninety-nine on the mountains and go in search of the one that went astray? And if he finds it, truly, I say to you, he rejoices over it more than over the ninety-nine that never went astray. So it is not the will of my Father who is in heaven that one of these little ones should perish. (Matt. 18:12-14)

The Lord takes care of His people, and we should too. But because of the selfish bent of our nature, it is a serious challenge to do so from our hearts, and do it in the right way. Additionally, Satan is at war with God's people, and he is trying to keep leaders from caring for them as they should. Such spiritual warfare is the reality in which we live, and that is one reason I like to use military illustrations so often in my teaching. The following is a good example of a leader who cared for the people under his authority.

Omar Bradley was one of the greatest American military commanders of World War II. He was a gifted strategist, able to foresee what the enemy might do and able to develop a winning battle plan – but that's not what made him great. He was a competent tactician, able to effectively execute orders and bring forces to bear in an efficient manner – nor was that what made him great. He was superb at the operational arts and was able to direct complicated operations, motivate subordinates, support his superiors, and cooperate with his peer officers – but that is not what made him great either.

As a career army officer and a West Pointer, Bradley was disappointed to have missed a field commission in World War I; he was kept busy training troops until the war's end. When World War II began, he chafed for a combat command, but he dutifully accepted one stateside post after another, training troops. Eventually, he earned the role of Commander of the First U.S. Army during Operation Overlord – the D-Day invasion of Normandy – second only to General Eisenhower, and wound up supervising more troops than any other general in American history. But even that is not what made him great.

Before being called to combat, Bradley was placed in charge of training the U.S. Army's Eighty-second and Twenty-eighth Infantry Divisions – huge bodies of troops who would be placed at the heart of the American war effort in the European theater. Bradley approached his command with commendable zeal and with the determination that his troops would be both motivated and protected as much as possible. To accomplish that goal, he made sure that all arriving recruits were welcomed to camp by a military band to boost morale. When they marched to their barracks, they were greeted by new uniforms, the best equipment available, and a hot meal. Bradley also implemented an innovative physical training program, which better prepared the citizen-soldiers of World War II for life in the field. His men knew that he cared for them, so they fought long and hard for him in return, and respected and loved him for the rest of their lives.

Other successful American commanders of World War II – General George Patton, for instance – achieved battlefield fame, but only Omar Bradley left a legacy as 'the soldier's general'. He did so by practicing the maxim that great leaders take care of their people. Not only do great leaders resolutely commit to achieving the mission, but they always strive to do what is best for those who serve under them.

Great Leaders Intentionally Produce Other Leaders

In November 1965, Lieutenant Colonel Harold 'Hal' Moore Jr. and the U.S. Seventh Cavalry's First Battalion were engaged in one of the opening battles of the Vietnam War. Surrounded by an estimated 4,000 North Vietnamese regulars at a jungle clearing called Landing Zone X-Ray, Moore's 450 soldiers were taking searing fire from all sides. Even with periodic American air support, his outnumbered troops faced annihilation.

Moore was determined that his men would survive, however, and he directed a heroic defense in what proved to be one of the fiercest battles of the war. He and his soldiers repulsed repeated assaults and inflicted severe casualties on the enemy until his battalion was finally relieved by reinforcements. The dramatic story is told in the 1992 best seller, *We Were Soldiers Once...and Young*, which was made into an acclaimed motion picture.[2]

Moore won the army's highest award, the Distinguished Service Cross, and eventually rose to the rank of lieutenant general. He was renowned for his superb leadership skills. A scene in the movie captured his foresight and grasp of leadership principles when Moore's character confronted a squad leader who had been unceremoniously 'killed' in a training exercise. 'You are dead,' Moore declared. 'Now, who do you have ready to take your place?' The scene reflects both the reality of warfare and our third maxim: *great leaders always prepare to reproduce and multiply themselves.*

In military warfare, a leader is always a target, and it's no different in spiritual warfare. Remember, Satan always has leaders in his crosshairs. Observe:

---

2. Harold Moore and Joseph Galloway, *We Were Soldiers Once...and Young: The Battle of La Drang, November 14-15, 1965* (Nashville: Flatsigned Press, 1992), p. 93.

Salvation is free
Discipleship costs
Leadership costs a lot more

There is always a price to pay in leadership, a principle affirmed in Zechariah 13:7: 'Strike the shepherd, and the sheep will be scattered.' The Bible teaches that Christians strive against the world, the flesh, and the devil – and all three forces incessantly attack leaders in particular. The world, especially contemporary American culture, constantly misrepresents the meaning of true leadership. Our flesh tempts us to shrink back in fear, strike out in anger, accommodate by appeasement, or isolate ourselves with legalism. Of course Satan is on the prowl for ways to attack Christian leaders at every opportunity. Jesus warned Peter (and us) that God's leaders are Satan's targets: 'Simon, Simon,' he said to the future leader, 'Behold, Satan demanded to have you [a plural pronoun in the Greek text], that he might sift you [plural] like wheat, but I have prayed for you [singular] that your faith may not fail.' (Luke 22:31-32)

Christ's words reveal that Satan 'prays' against leaders and Satan 'preys' on leaders. The Enemy's design at that moment in history was to eradicate all twelve future leaders, but even though they faltered in the moment of trial, the Lord preserved both their faith and their future leadership. And if the extra-biblical historical accounts are correct, they ultimately sacrificed their own lives as martyrs for the cause of Christ, obviously no longer controlled by fear.

There was one disciple, however, who turned away from Christ and never did experience repentance and restoration: Judas, Christ's betrayer, ended up taking his own life in regret and despair. Peter did something just as bad, or perhaps even worse, by denying Christ three times. But unlike Judas, Peter ended up becoming a legendary leader in the church. What was the difference between the two men? I believe that it was the intercession of Christ, who said to Peter, 'I have prayed for you' (Luke 22:32). And I am so encouraged to know that the same loving Savior is still 'interceding for us' today (Rom. 8:34). As Hebrews 7:25 says: 'Consequently,

He is able to save to the uttermost those who draw near to God through Him, since He always lives to make intercession for them.'

> Salvation is free. Discipleship costs. Leadership costs a lot more.

Knowing that fighting the good fight requires a multitude of leaders and that leaders sometimes become casualties, great leaders are those who intentionally reproduce themselves. Eventually all of us will be called home, so who will be there to take our place? Paul had Timothy and others prepared to replace him. Elijah prepared Elisha. Moses prepared Joshua and Caleb. Jesus had the Seventy, the Twelve, and the Three prepared when He ascended to heaven. Great leaders don't leave behind a vacuum waiting to be filled by the devil's counterfeits, but they work hard at multiplying qualified replacements who are ready to expand the kingdom of God throughout the world.

My understanding of this crucial maxim once prompted a memorable conversation with my son. As he neared graduation from college, I shared some family history that I hoped would make a point. I admitted to my son that I had failed as his father many times, and I asked him to forgive me. Then I explained to him that despite my failings, he had been given a better father than I had been given. I quickly explained that the same had been true for me – I had been given a better father than my dad had been given. And his father, who was my grandfather, had been a better father than the father he had been given. I knew this from the history of spiritual growth in our family, which had occurred as a result of Christian discipleship over many generations and God's merciful faithfulness within a covenant family.

That's the way it should be, I told my son. Those who follow in a line of believers should always reach a higher level of spiritual maturity than those who came before them. That's what good discipleship and effective leadership will produce. By the grace of God and the proper exercise of disciplined leadership, my son and daughters will go even farther than I in their walk with Christ and service for Him. Therefore, our family will continue to be blessed by the truth of Psalm 16:6: 'The lines have fallen for me in pleasant places; indeed, I have a beautiful inheritance.'

In the same way, the church as the family of God must be committed to the reproduction and multiplication of leadership. One of the main reasons good churches decline in subsequent generations is because they have failed to disciple effective leaders who can take the church and its mission forward to extend the kingdom of God. Satan gladly fills the leadership vacuum with false teachers who cause the devolution of the culture and a death spiral in the ministry. So leaders who want to see God's blessings extend 'to a thousand generations' must commit themselves to the biblical principle of leadership multiplication.

The mark of great leaders is not the number of their followers, but how they attract and intentionally develop the next generation of leaders.

Great Leaders Wisely Avoid Common Failures

Those first three maxims – *great leaders know their mission and are unalterably committed to achieving it; great leaders take care of their people;* and *great leaders intentionally reproduce leaders* – seem so obvious upon reflection. So why are they not practiced more often? The answer is that distraction, disillusionment, and other dangers get in the way. Great leaders, on the other hand, are aware of the potential roadblocks and avoid them at all costs.

Failure to keep the main thing as the main thing

A salesman was driving along a road one day, and in a field nearby he saw a young boy with a bow and arrow standing beside a barn, which had numerous arrows stuck in the bull's-eye of numerous targets. The salesman stopped to watch this presumably expert archer. The young man strung the bow and launched another arrow into the side of the barn. He then approached the barn, picked up a bucket of paint and a paint brush, and proceeded to paint a target around the arrow.

That illustrates a problem with many leaders today. They shoot multiple arrows of activity and then celebrate how much work they have done, whether or not it actually advances a worthwhile mission. Do you know your target – your mission – and is it consistent with God's Word and your calling? If so, do you maintain the personal discipline to keep that particular mission a priority? You are not called to meet every need.

Are you spread too thin on too many fronts to effectively fulfill your God-given mission? Don't be distracted by momentary fascinations and fads. Don't be diverted by prolonged 'emergencies'. Don't be detoured by the tyranny of what others declare as urgent. Don't be impulsive; instead be thoughtfully and prayerfully deliberate. Be responsive, but do not be easily detoured. Don't let even good things obscure the more important things. More than one gifted ministry leader has lost sight of the defined mission by becoming repeatedly enamored by every possibility, distracted by unrelated issues, or even lured by opportunities for personal acclaim and advancement.

Following that kind of leadership is like being in a car with a sixteen-year-old who has not yet learned how to drive properly. The vehicle careens from one side of the lane to the other, erratically increases speed, suddenly brakes to a halt, then zooms forward again. The passengers become unnerved, exhausted, and hopeless of ever experiencing a steady ride. Eventually they will abandon either the vehicle or its driver, and much time and distance is lost.

Keep the main thing as the main thing! Your God-given mission must be guarded as sacred, and you must both embrace it and be absorbed with it. Great leaders are fixed on the target God has established for them.

Failure to maintain the integrity of the message

An essential part of the mission God has given to Christian leaders is the communication of Gospel truth, and it is far too easy to become imbalanced one way or another in that task.

On the one hand, we must be careful to avoid a *destructive dogmatism* that treats all doctrines as if they were of equal importance. 'Keeping the main thing the main thing' applies to this issue as well, because although all scriptural truths are important, some are primary, some are secondary, and some are tertiary. In the primary and essential doctrines of Scripture we must be clear and unyielding. In secondary and tertiary ones we must practice charity as people grapple with them, realizing those issues are not essential in terms of salvation.

Therefore, we need to major on the majors and minor on the minors. That does not mean compromising on what we believe, but it does mean being understanding and respectful, especially when dealing with secondary and tertiary biblical issues. For instance, one's perspective on the mode and subjects of baptism is not going to affect his or her eternal destiny. Therefore, while we should study those issues and decide what we personally believe about them, we should recognize that good Christians have differed on them and be extra patient with one another as we work through those differences.

On the other hand, we must also avoid a *permissive pragmatism* that is equally harmful. It is actually possible to commit primary errors in how we deal with secondary doctrines, like placing peace before purity or watering down the truth to attract more followers. All doctrines may not be equally important, but all doctrines *are* important, because God cared enough to reveal them in His Word. You should not be afraid to say what you believe about them after careful study, and never compromise the integrity of the biblical message to fulfill your mission.

Great leaders know how to stay both on mission and on message at the same time. Is that easy in today's culture? No, of course not. It requires knowledge of the Word, commitment to the mission, fidelity to the message, and humble reliance on the grace of God, while treating others with respect and dignity. Remember that the Great Commission, the marching orders for every Christian leader, requires us to teach *all* that Christ has commanded us (Matt. 28:19-20). The Apostle Paul declared that he was 'innocent of the blood of all' because he had publicly and privately declared to them the whole counsel of God (Acts 20:26).

Teaching all of God's Word means that we should reflect its priorities by emphasizing the essential and primary doctrines. But we cannot neglect the secondary and tertiary doctrines and still fulfill the mission we have been given by Christ.

> The mark of great leaders is not the number of their followers, but how they attract and intentionally develop the next generation of leaders.

Failure to be courageous

It is easy to identify leaders who are governed by fear of failure. They become indecisive or hesitant, and they may even attempt to pass decisions or responsibilities on to others.

A question that I like to ask when interviewing someone for a leadership position is, 'Will you please identify three instances in which you've failed and what you've learned from each failure?' It's a revealing question for a leader. If you have never experienced a failure, you have never really exercised leadership. An absence of failure usually reflects an unwillingness to take risks because of a fear of failure. But great leaders do not always 'play it safe'. Leadership requires risks. Of course, a ministry replete with continual failures reflects other problems, and a responsible leader is not rash or impetuous.

A humble willingness to be decisive and aggressive – prayerfully and thoughtfully – is inherent to leadership, and sometimes it results in failure. A great leader then seizes that moment for personal development, turning the experience into an instructive learning experience.

If you have a debilitating fear of failure, surrender it to the Lord and ask Him for courage to lead others forward in a responsible manner with your confidence in the strength and might of your God. As the famed Civil War General Thomas J. 'Stonewall' Jackson was known for saying, 'Never take counsel from your fears.'

Failure to take care of yourself

'Keep a close watch on *yourself* and on the teaching,' Paul said to his protégé Timothy (1 Tim. 4:16). He also told him: 'Train *yourself* for godliness.' (1 Tim. 4:7) And before he wrote his famous words in 2 Timothy 2:2 about multiplying other leaders, he first said this: 'You then, my child, be strengthened by the grace that is in

Christ Jesus.' (2 Tim. 2:1) He then goes on to add: 'And what you have heard from me in the presence of many witnesses entrust to faithful men, who will be able to teach others also.' (v. 2) But the order of the commands implies that Timothy would not be effective in training others unless he himself was 'strengthened by the grace that is in Christ Jesus' (v. 1).

Leaders cannot focus on their mission, care for their people, or reproduce and multiply if they do not take care of themselves. Spiritual care is the first priority. Practice what you preach. Do not neglect a regular time with the Lord in prayer and the Word. Ministry preparation – preaching, teaching, serving – is not the same as personal time with the Lord. Nourish yourself spiritually. Do not neglect to confess your sins and receive the blessing and empowerment of God's forgiveness. Avoid compromise, violating your conscience, and falling into patterns of sin. Maintain your witness with a faithful lifestyle. Strive before the Lord to live above reproach in a way that honors your Savior.

Also, take care of yourself physically and emotionally. 'You shall not put the Lord your God to the test,' as we're reminded in Matthew 4:7 (quoting Deut. 6:16). As a leader, you are required to care for your body as the Lord's temple just as everyone else must. Follow a healthful diet. Exercise. Plan free personal time in your schedule. Spend time with your family, enjoy a hobby, get a healthful amount of sleep, avoid stress. Do what is necessary and helpful to take care of yourself. Remember that Christian leadership is not a sprint – it's a marathon. Pace yourself so you can finish strong physically, emotionally, and spiritually.

Failure to learn lessons or receive discipline

Finally, leaders fail when they become prideful or arrogant. Show me a leader who refuses to learn from his mistakes or who refuses to humbly accept discipline, and I will show you a leader who is racing toward failure. You cannot lead others if you yourself are unwilling to be led or unwilling to learn. Often, our greatest learning experiences come through our failures – and a leader must be willing to humbly admit error and learn from it. Sometimes we must receive discipline from our peers or our superiors. *Many* times in life we will be disciplined by the Lord. This is how we grow, and it is a gift of God's grace.

Remember this admonition: 'My son, do not regard lightly the discipline of the Lord, nor be weary when reproved by Him. For the Lord disciplines the one he loves, and chastises every son whom he receives ... For the moment all discipline seems painful rather than pleasant, but later it yields the peaceful fruit of righteousness to those who have been trained by it.' (Heb. 12:5-6, 11; quoting Prov. 3:11-12)

The Christian leader needs to be constantly experiencing the grace of God by surrendering to the Holy Spirit and maintaining the heart and lifestyle of a learner. A great leader will invariably have a voracious appetite to continually grow in the Lord and to lead others by example.

Great leaders know their mission and are unalterably committed to achieving it. Great leaders take care of their people. Great leaders intentionally produce leaders. Great leaders wisely avoid common failures.

We want to see the world filled with men and women who are great leaders according to God's definition. If this happens the world will be 'turned upside down' as it once was by the leaders that Christ Himself trained. If you want to be a part of this movement of God's Spirit, then seek to be a great leader yourself by practicing the biblical principles in these first four chapters, as we have described the biblical definition of true leadership. Then you will be able to be used by God in the next dimension of 3D Leadership, which is the *development* of more leaders by individuals and by the church.

When a Godly leader shows up, things change. When he or she develops other Godly leaders, the effect is exponential and the whole world can be changed for the glory of our triune God.

Questions for Thought and Discussion

1) What examples have you seen, good and bad, that support the adage 'leadership works' (or to put it in scriptural terms from Matthew 10:25, 'the disciple becomes like his teacher')?

2) Do you have a clearly understood mission in each of the leadership opportunities you have been given? If you do, how can you better communicate that mission to those you lead?

3) Read chapters 15 and 16 of Romans, and notice the various ways that Paul demonstrated his sincere care for the people in that church. He was a great leader, and his words in those passages are inspired by God, so we can learn a lot from them.

4) Are you intentionally reproducing yourself by training others in the ministries you lead? If not, identify at least one person in each of them, and consider how you can raise them up to carry on the ministry when you're gone.

5) Have you fallen into any of the failures discussed in the last part of this chapter? If so, take some time to plan and pray about how you can improve in those areas.

3D Leadership
Part 2

The Second Dimension – Developing Leaders

Chapter 5

Thermometer or Thermostat?

TURN on the TV. Pick up a newspaper. Listen to the radio. Do an Internet search for any subject. You'll quickly realize that American leadership is increasingly composed of 'thermometer leaders' rather than 'thermostat leaders'.

A thermometer has one use: to sense and then communicate the room temperature. A thermostat, on the other hand, is used to change the temperature. A thermostat will measure the temperature of a room and then adjust it as needed.

As contemporary American culture continues its death spiral, thermostat leaders are desperately needed – leaders who will help transform the culture from death to life. But while we have few thermostat leaders, we're inundated with legions of thermometer leaders. They are everywhere – in politics, education, the arts, and sadly, even the church. They reflect our declining culture by absorbing its fascination with and addiction to greed, sexual immorality, consumerism, narcissism, and self-promotion. They propagate the culture of death in a variety of ways: abortion, euthanasia, drugs, sexual promiscuity, and violence. But what if the church began developing and deploying thermostat leaders in our communities, at all levels of government and in every realm of society? Our world would definitely change. The only question is how quickly it would happen.

Three Thermostat Leaders

The old adage is true: One person *can* make a difference and, if committed to the Lord, a significant difference.

An ambitious young man named George called out to God, 'O Lord, I want to know about you. I want to know about your creation. O God, I want to know about the universe.' He sensed that the Lord's answer to his prayer was, 'No, George, the universe is too big for you.' He conceded that truth, but prayed again, 'All right, Lord, if not the universe, teach me all about the earth.' Again he sensed the Lord telling him, 'No George, that is still too big for you.' Exasperated, he cried out, 'God, I want to help my people. Will you teach me about a peanut?'

And God granted his request. George – an extraordinary chemist, educator, artist, and agriculturalist – transformed the South and affected the entire nation because he was humble enough to submit his will to God's. George Washington Carver became internationally famous as the prodigious inventor of a multitude of uses of the tiny peanut. One of my prized possessions hanging in my study, is a picture of him working in a modest laboratory at Tuskegee University.

Carver identified more than three hundred uses for the lowly Southern peanut – from peanut butter to cosmetics – and more than a hundred uses for the sweet potato. His commitment was not without distractions – some quite flattering and tempting. The acclaimed fellow inventor and scientist Thomas Edison offered him a prestigious job with a huge salary as did pioneer automaker Henry Ford. Carver declined both. Why would he turn down both of these offers, which were reported to be for over $100,000 annually? Because Carver wanted to be faithful to the Lord's call upon his life, which was more important than personal advancement, acclaim, or affluence. His calling was to help lift the people of the South from agricultural and economic ruin, and to help prepare the first generation of freed slaves for a new life. George Washington Carver's life's work and research was intentionally based on biblical principles.

George Washington Carver gave up fame and fortune, content with a salary of $1,500 a year. He teamed up with another former slave, Booker T. Washington, to establish Alabama's Tuskegee University. For Carver it wasn't about money. It wasn't about fame. It was about obedience to the Lord and to his calling. The result was an innovative educational institution, a rescued and transformed society, and a leadership model that is still affecting our culture. That is the essence of thermostat leadership.

George Washington Carver's love for the Lord and his drive to serve were matched in kind by his colleague, Booker T. Washington. His calling? He was determined to educate a generation of former slaves and their children, and he did so from a biblically-based perspective. He believed former slaves and their offspring were not a burden to American society but an untapped asset. He believed that an emphasis on Christian education and character could enable those who had been on the bottom rung of society to become genuine achievers and productive citizens.

Booker T. Washington was not waiting for someone to give him and this newly emancipated generation of African-Americans a seat at the table. He had a vision that his people would make the table and sell the table, and that their character and conduct would, of necessity, create a desire to invite his students to the table as honored guests. Not only did he believe that – he accomplished it personally. It wasn't easy for a black American to take a public position in those days, but Washington followed his calling, turning down multiple lucrative offers like his partner Carver had.

Speaking of being invited to a table as an honored guest, Booker T. Washington so impressed President Theodore Roosevelt that 'Teddy' invited him to the White House. That momentous event was the first time an African-American had ever been honored to sit at the table of a White House luncheon. It was a bold and courageous act of leadership by Roosevelt. News of the event sparked a media outcry, but the former Rough Rider was undeterred, and afterward developed a friendship with Washington.

Roosevelt made Washington an influential member of his unofficial circle of advisors – his 'kitchen cabinet' – and turned to him for advice on securing qualified leadership for appointments in the South. It was an important precedent for the nation, and Roosevelt needed sacrificial courage to do it.

That's the kind of leadership we want to develop in the church today. None of these three men – Carver, Washington, or Roosevelt – was a thermometer leader, playing it safe and fitting into the culture. They were thermostat leaders who fulfilled their mission and calling with integrity. Our nation was changed for the better, and we are still being blessed by them to this day. All three men were Christians, and like other Christian leaders in the Bible and history they embodied qualities that all thermostat leaders have that form the basis of a plan for developing them in the church today.

> 'Thermometer' leaders merely reflect the state of our declining culture; 'thermostat' leaders work hard to change it.

Three Essential Qualities of Thermostat Leadership

Determined, focused, and principled leadership refuses to be narcissistic, self-promoting, or greed-driven. Instead, it seeks to be faithful to the Lord and serve others, and in doing so can change the landscape of life. But how can we develop such leaders and what is a biblical curriculum for doing so? One day while reading Hebrews 13:7, which could be characterized as a 'followership' verse, I was struck not only by the meaningful exhortation to followers but also by the embedded presuppositions about the leaders whom Christians should follow. The verse says: 'Remember your leaders, those who spoke to you the Word of God. Consider the outcome of their way of life, imitate their faith.'

Clearly that text is exhorting followers to remember their leaders, follow them, listen to them, and imitate them. But notice the three assumptions about these Christian leaders. First, their *character* and conduct was worthy of imitation by their followers. Secondly, they could speak the Word of God because they knew the Word of God. You cannot teach what you do not know. The *content* of biblical truth was well understood in their minds. Thirdly, they were able to lead because they had *competency*. These three elements are presented elsewhere in Scripture as essential to the development of principle-driven, influential thermostat leaders.

Character

Leaders whom we are to imitate must have lives worthy of imitation. Therefore, a Christian leader must have Godly character. It is the foundation of the other two elements. Leadership content and competencies are meaningless without it. Unfortunately, I have seen churches and other organizations destroyed by ministry leaders who are theologically knowledgeable (content) and/or personally charismatic and effective (competency), because of a lack of Christian character. Godly character is driven by the grace of God, focused on the glory of God, empowered by the Spirit of God, and defined by the Word of God – all the while propelled by the love of God. Character counts, and one of the greatest truths I have learned about it is this: *Circumstances do not determine your character, they reveal it, and become the occasion to refine it.*

A classic example of that maxim is General Robert E. Lee, a devout believer who felt compelled to defend his state in the Civil War even though he opposed secession and despised slavery. He was left with practically nothing but hardship when the war ended. His home, Arlington Plantation, which overlooked Washington, D.C., from the Virginia side of the Potomac River, had been confiscated by the federal government and turned into a military cemetery. His wife had become an invalid. One of his daughters had died. He had suffered a series of heart attacks that left him in questionable health, and he had no foreseeable source of income. A prominent insurance company offered him a huge salary simply for the use of his name as an endorsement, but Lee declined, saying that his fame as a military commander had come at the cost of many soldiers' lives and he would not take advantage of them.

He also said, 'my name is not for sale at any price.'[1] I often think of that whenever I encounter a mindless celebrity product endorsement. Instead, he accepted a comparatively small salary of $1,500 a year as president of Washington College – now Washington and Lee University – a small, obscure Southern college in Virginia's Shenandoah Valley. There, he committed himself to instilling in young people a character-based education rooted in Christian ethics, which he believed could help restore a broken nation. Meanwhile, he set a personal example of reconciliation and reunion.

---

1. J. William Jones, *The Life and Letters of Robert Edward Lee: Soldier and Man* (New York: Neale, 1906), p. 445.

Lee's character made him a success in his peacetime calling, earned him the respect of the entire nation – North and South, which was demonstrated on multiple occasions even before he took the job at Washington College. After he surrendered his army at Appomattox in April 1865, signaling to all other Southern commanders that the war was over, Lee returned to his wartime home in Richmond. He worshiped each Lord's Day at St Paul's Protestant Episcopal Church, pushing his wife in a wheelchair. Services at St Paul's were racially integrated, but the seating was segregated, with white worshipers seated on the ground floor and black worshipers seated in the church balcony. Sunday worship ended in communion, and the practice was for each group to sing hymns while the other took communion – black worshipers singing while white worshipers were administered the Lord's Supper, then whites singing while blacks partook of the table.

Richmond was occupied by Northern troops at the time, and one June Sunday in 1865 two Northern soldiers attended worship to make sure that the pastor prayed publicly for the president of the United States – which he did. But they also had another purpose in mind. When the time came for communion to be administered, the two soldiers came forward with a former slave, obviously intending to evoke an incident.

As they led the man to kneel at the communion rail, the entire congregation – white and black – froze in place. A tense silence gripped the congregation. No one knew what to do until Robert E. Lee rose from his seat, walked with measured military cadence down the marble-floored aisle, knelt beside the man, and put his hand on his shoulder. Then the two – black and white – took communion together.

Afterward, the entire congregation came forward from both floors and received the Lord's Supper on a glorious day in the life of St Paul's Church. Several worshipers recorded the incident in their personal journals. What could have been a disastrous confrontation was transformed on that day into a celebration of the love of Christ, regardless of race – all because of the Christ-centered character of one man.

Circumstances do not dictate character, but reveal it and become the occasion to refine it.

Content

The second essential element in developing a thermostat leader is *content* – a strong knowledge of sound, biblical theology. Too many church leaders today have adopted a 'cafeteria theology' – picking a little of what they like here and a little more there and ignoring the rest. A Christian leader cannot do that, but instead must embrace a theology that respects the Word of God as 'verbal, plenary inspiration' that is fully inerrant right down to the choice and order of every word. Sound theology requires us to frame everything by Scripture – to consistently look at everything through a biblical worldview. To live the Bible, we must know it. To know it, we must study it. That is why Paul commands his pastoral apprentice to become 'a worker who has no need to be ashamed, rightly handling the word of truth' (2 Tim. 2:15).

Christian leadership begins with the leader's having assurance of personal salvation – that he or she has received Jesus Christ as Lord and Savior (2 Tim. 3:14-15). A genuine Christian leader accepts the Word of God from Genesis through Revelation as inerrant in its original autographs; life-changing in practice; and authoritative as well as transformational over any and all human endeavors (2 Tim. 3:16-17).

A true Christian leader also has a heart that is surrendered to live for Christ and pursues a growing, consistent lifestyle that displays the evidence of salvation and a maturing walk with the Lord (2 Tim. 2:22). Spiritual warfare for such a leader is inevitable, because Satan will continually seek to undermine the character of Christians, especially leaders, with temptations to indolence, immorality, and insubordination. We flee Satan's temptations and we stand firm by *knowing* and *obeying* the Word of God in order to put on the 'armor of God' (Eph. 6:11) while making full use of the 'weapons of God' (2 Cor. 10:3-6).

Following is a list of some key areas of theology and Bible content that need to be incorporated in the development of a Christian leader:

- The doctrine of Scripture
- The doctrine of God

- The doctrine of man (in creation, fall, and redemption)
- The Gospel
- The doctrines of church, state, family, etc.

> 'Remember your leaders, those who spoke to you the Word of God. Consider the outcome of their way of life, imitate their faith' (Heb. 13:7).

Also crucial to a sound theology is an understanding and reliance on the biblical doctrine of Divine Providence. This essential truth is succinctly stated in Romans 8:28: 'And we know that for those who love God all things work together for good, for those who are called according to his purpose.' Behind this doctrine is the loving smile of the Sovereign God. He does not promise that everything that comes into our lives as believers in this sinful world will be good, but that He will personally work all things together for our good. Trusting in the sovereignty of God enables a leader to avoid self-adulation and exaltation in success. Rather he or she will give glory to God, knowing that the victory came from the hand of the Lord. In defeat, on the other hand, leaders are kept from the pit of despair by the doctrine of providence because they know that God is also at work in the adversities of life. Praising and thanking God in both the good times and bad enables a leader, and every other Christian, to grow in confidence and contentment.

When we embrace Divine Providence in our lives, God blesses us with stability and peace, removes anxieties and fears, and shields us from self-centeredness, enabling us to glorify God alone. Here is an example – again from the Civil War – of how trusting in the sovereignty of a providential God brings peace that surpasses all understanding, so that one's Christian character can remain steadfast in the midst of any circumstance.

When he was shot down in the 1864 assault at Petersburg, thirty-five-year-old Union Colonel Joshua Lawrence Chamberlain was already a war hero. By vocation he was a teacher, a professor of theology and rhetoric at Maine's Bowdoin College. He had left the classroom to join the Northern war effort as a volunteer officer in the Twentieth Maine Infantry. He proved to be a natural leader, surviving some of the war's worst fighting at Antietam and Fredericksburg, and was promoted to colonel and commander of the regiment in time for the battle of Gettysburg. There, Chamberlain's leadership and command decisions helped save the battle for the Northern forces, and eventually led him to be known throughout the North as the 'hero of Gettysburg'.

A year later, while commanding a brigade of federal troops at the siege of Petersburg, he was ordered to lead his brigade in a desperate assault against the Confederate line. Some officers believed it was a foolish and hopeless assignment: the assault route lay across a broad, open killing field, and massed fire from the Southern lines had already felled countless Northern troops.

'My heart dropped to my shoes,' one of Chamberlain's fellow officers later recalled about the moment the order was issued.[2] Despite the deadly odds, Chamberlain courageously led his troops forward. They were immediately struck by a searing torrent of enemy fire. The assault disintegrated, and Chamberlain, still holding his sword and the colors of his battalion, was shot down at the head of his troops. Dragged out of the line of fire by his men, he was carried to a field hospital. Army surgeons tried to save his life, but finally concluded that his case was hopeless. Nothing else could be done, they told the young officer, explaining that he would soon die. So Chamberlain asked for a scrap of paper and a pencil, and wrote a goodbye note to his wife back home in Maine:

> My darling wife I am lying mortally wounded the doctors think, but my mind & heart are at peace. Jesus Christ is my all-sufficient savior. I go to him. God bless & keep & comfort you, precious one, you have been a precious wife to me. To know & love you makes life & death beautiful. Cherish the darlings & give my love to all the dear ones. Do not grieve too much for me. We shall all soon meet. Live for the children. Give my dearest love to Father, mother and Sallie & John.

---

2. Joshua L. Chamberlain to 'My Darling Wife,' 19 June 1864, Joshua L. Chamberlain Papers, Special Collections, Hawthorne-Longfellow Library, Bowdoin College.

Oh how happy to feel yourself forgiven. God bless you ever more precious, precious one. Ever yours, Lawrence[3]

Notice that he expressed no bitterness, no second-guessing, no recrimination toward his commanders. His words were few, but reflected the confidence and contentment that comes with assurance of salvation and a belief in God's Divine Providence.

Incidentally, Chamberlain surprised the physicians and survived his wound, returned home to his wife and family, eventually served four terms as governor of Maine, and lived until age ninety-four. Divine Providence had a different plan for him than what the doctors said in the field hospital that day. And a reliance on that doctrine, when properly understood, allows a Christian leader to stabilize in days of defeat and adversity as well as to remain in touch with reality when victorious.

Competency

A third quality we need to develop in church leaders is the skill and ability to fulfill their ministries with excellence. The inculcation of Christian *character* rooted in sound biblical *content* produces a trustworthy *competency* in a Christian leader. And competent leaders affect everything around them – not as thermometer leaders but as thermostat leaders. How specifically can they do it? A thermostat leader will be used by the Lord to change the lives of God's people by *modeling, mentoring, motivating, managing,* and *ministering.* These are the skills that need to be developed.

A thermostat leader will make an impact on those who look to him by *modeling* – consistently demonstrating growth and maturity, with a measure of transparency and permeated by humility. Why transparency? Because a Christian leader never pretends perfection – only Christ is perfect – but the leader *can and should* model spiritual growth: acknowledging the common struggles of life, readily confessing sin, making the improvements that reflect a heart that is surrendered and growing in grace. Transparency and a Christ-centered life of character yields a powerful model.

---

3. ibid.

Followers are taught and strengthened by exposure to a leader who is sensitive to sin, careful in conduct, and humbly committed to honoring the Lord with a faithful witness. Humility is also a major key to all of this, because Christian leaders realize that they are what they are only by the grace of God, so their progress in the Christian life is never a cause for boasting or relying on themselves.

An unforgettable example of such modeling is the sixteenth-century ministry of William Tyndale, the English clergyman who was put to death during the Reformation for translating the Bible into the English language. Persecuted and driven from his native England into hiding on the European continent, Tyndale courageously continued his work until the first English New Testament was printed in 1526. When most of the copies were obtained and burned by church officials, Tyndale promptly went back to work and produced another printing. Eventually, however, while working on a translation of the Old Testament, William Tyndale was betrayed, captured, and executed. His last words were 'Lord! Open the King of England's eyes.'

But as a believer and a translator, Tyndale had faithfully served as a model for one of his assistants – a protégé named Miles Coverdale. Valiantly and skillfully, Coverdale completed Tyndale's translation of the Old Testament and arranged the first printing of the entire Bible in English – the Coverdale Bible – in 1535. Copies flooded England, and the British people embraced it. Popular demand for the English Bible soon became so strong that King Henry finally ordered an 'authorized version'. It became known as the 'Great Bible', which led the way to the most popular English translation in history (the King James Bible or *Authorised Version* of 1611), and was providentially printed by the man who had learned from the model of William Tyndale – Miles Coverdale.

> Christian leaders realize that they are what they are only by the grace of God, so their progress in the Christian life is never a cause for boasting or relying on themselves.

In addition to modeling, Christian leaders *mentor*. They teach, coach, and instruct. They will find various ways to do that, but they will always attempt to help others identify and respond biblically to the issues of life. Effective mentoring requires committing to spend time with those who are being mentored, and that requires patience. Patience requires a genuine love for them, and it leads to perseverance with them. It often involves forgiveness as well, when those who are being coached fail, falter, and at times wander.

A thermostat leader will also be a *motivator*. Motivators know when to speak, what to say and how to say it, and they know what to do and what *not* to do in order to inspire their disciples. They avoid crossing the line from uplifting motivation into destructive manipulation. For all believers, the love of Christ that 'controls us' (2 Cor. 5:14) is the primary motivation for every aspect of life, though, to a lesser degree, we are influenced by other valid motivational dynamics.

As a parent, I quickly learned that all three of my children were different and were motivated by different methods. One child was motivated by competition. If I simply asked, 'Do you think you can do this?' it would probably be done. Another child was motivated by the quest for excellence. 'Do you think you can beat your old time at running the 3200 meters?' I might ask – and the race was on. The third child was motivated by relationships and affirmation. Doing things together provided incentive, and genuine affirmation of each valid achievement became a springboard to the next one.

In the final analysis, a motivator appeals to the great aspirations and ideals of life, while introducing followers to the inexhaustible power that comes only through a relationship with Jesus Christ. 'Apart from me you can do nothing,' He says in John 15:5 – and Paul says: 'I can do all things through him who strengthens me.' (Phil. 4:13) That is the confidence we have as believers, and it is not just in success that we can honor Christ. It is also in the way we handle disappointments and defeats.

Thermostat leaders understand that we should strive to live for Christ in all honorable endeavors in the messiness of a fallen world where we encounter good times and bad times. They motivate others to trust in the wisdom, grace, and power of God, to 'stay the course' and take life to the next level for the glory of God.

A thermostat leader also strives to be an effective *manager*. Granted, not every leader is a gifted manager – and certainly not every gifted manager is a leader – but biblical leaders must make sure that those in their care have the benefits of effective administration. Sometimes this is simply a matter of responsible delegation, but it is absolutely essential, and the ultimate responsibility for it lies with the leader. Motivation inspires ardor, but management is necessary for order. Motivation produces passion. Management produces precision. Both are necessary for effective, balanced thermostat leadership.

My maternal grandfather was a memorable example of management competency. When I was a boy, Granddaddy could fix anything, but I was puzzled by the way he approached a challenge. Every time he began a project, he would first sit down with a pencil and paper, silently thinking and scribbling for what seemed like hours. I finally asked him one time why we couldn't just *get started*. 'We're not ready yet,' he told me. 'I'm studying on it.' Of course, I was impatient, ready to plunge in, but after a while I came to understand what he meant by 'studying on it'.

He carefully planned each job. Before he invested a moment of work on the task, he figured out what needed to be done and what materials were necessary to do it. Had a job been left to me, I would have repeatedly climbed up and down a ladder because of all the things I had forgotten to bring to the task. When my grandfather went up a ladder to do a job, it took one trip. He had everything he needed because he had 'studied on it'.

Management skills are crucial for leadership because they dramatically increase our effectiveness. Effective leaders first learn to manage themselves and then bring thoughtful administration and its blessings to the task of leadership. They 'study on it'. The result is that the job gets done with integrity and insight and those engaged encounter minimal frustrations and distractions.

Finally, thermostat leaders must be *ministers* – they must have a servant's heart. The thirteenth chapter of John says that Peter protested when Jesus began to wash His disciples' feet in the upper room on the eve of the crucifixion. Jesus listened, addressed Peter's objections, and then finished the task. One by one, He washed the feet of everyone who was present. Then He issued a key command to all His followers for all time, a call to servanthood: 'If I then, your Lord and Teacher, have washed your feet,' He said, 'you also ought to wash one another's feet.' (John 13:14)

When I graduated from Westminster Seminary South, which was then called the Florida Theological Center, I remember the sense of accomplishment that I felt when walking across the stage to receive my diploma – and the final lesson imparted to me by the school. The dean of faculty gave me my diploma, shook my hand, and put the Master of Divinity hood over my shoulders. Then he handed me a towel bearing my initials, which hangs in my office today.

'You have now graduated with a theological degree, and you are ready for a call to the pastorate,' the dean said. 'This seminary's objective is done. You are equipped and knowledgeably qualified. In fact, you are equipped and qualified for the greatest privilege of all – the Gospel ministry. Now, here is your towel. You are qualified to wash the feet of the saints.'

The Word of God calls us to be servant leaders. We lead by serving. And that is one of the key differences between a thermostat leader and a thermometer leader. It is not easy to practice servant-hood, but that is the calling of a biblical leader, and is the kind of leadership so desperately needed in American culture today.

In summary, a thermostat leader is one with *character*, who applies sound theological *content* in a way that yields a *competent* ministry. He is one who *models, mentors, motivates, manages, and ministers* – all with the heart of a servant. Challenging? Absolutely. Impossible? Not at all – this is God's way, revealed in God's Word; and what God requires of us He will enable us to do. When hearts are surrendered in humble obedience, out of love for Christ and a desire to serve Him, God can and will produce leaders who will rise above the lukewarm tendencies of our culture and raise its spiritual temperature until multitudes are on fire for Christ.

That's the kind of leadership we need to develop in the church and society. So how does it happen in the lives of aspiring leaders? In the next chapter, we will learn more about how they can *be developed* in those areas of life – especially the all-important foundational aspect of personal character.

Questions for Thought and Discussion

1) What are some other examples, besides the three men mentioned at the beginning of this chapter, of 'thermostat leaders' who have changed their cultures rather than merely conforming to them?

2) What are some difficult circumstances you have faced in your life, and what did they reveal about your character?

3) What is Divine Providence, and how has understanding and relying upon it helped you in those difficult circumstances? Or how could it have?

4) How competent are you currently in your leadership abilities, according to the descriptions in this chapter? What could you do to improve them?

5) What are some good things that could happen to our culture if we had more thermostat leaders? Take some time to pray that God would use you and others in those ways.

Chapter 6

The Example of the Greatest Leader

ARE leaders born or made? Is it by nature or nurture?
The answer is 'Yes!' It is both. Some families seem to
have an undiscovered genetic strain that produces generations
of leaders. Others rise from a leaderless heritage. Leaders are
affected by family history and environment, but leadership can
also be learned. For example, not every man claims to be a gifted
leader, yet the Bible clearly teaches that every husband and father
is called to spiritually lead his family. And every believer – man
and woman alike – is called to 'lead' others to Christ. So those
called to leadership who are not natural leaders can still seek to
be faithful and effective by humbly and intentionally cultivating
leadership skills and insights from others.

The New Testament books of 1 and 2 Timothy were inspired by
the Holy Spirit and penned by the Apostle Paul to give his protégé
Timothy the leadership instruction necessary to carry on Paul's
ministry after his death. The book of 1 Timothy also contains
the basics of the church revitalization ministry Timothy was to
implement at Ephesus including Christ-centered and Gospel-
driven preaching and teaching, prayer, leadership, evangelism,
confessional unity, and worship.[1] Paul's final letter was 2 Timothy,
which he may have written hours before he was executed outside
Rome. Just as Elijah passed the mantle of leadership to Elisha in the

---

1. See Harry L. Reeder III with Dave Swavely, *From Embers to a Flame: How
God Can Revitalize Your Church* (P&R Publishing, 2008).

Old Testament, so Paul did the same to Timothy in that pastoral epistle. What is abundantly clear is that in his 'last words' found in 2 Timothy he packaged the biblical model of '3D leadership' for his 'son in the faith': he had *defined* leadership for Timothy, he had *developed* Timothy as a leader, and with his final letter he prepared Timothy to be *deployed* as a leader.

As he did so, he exhorted Timothy to develop his leadership skills: 'Fan into flame the gift of God, which is in you through the laying on of my hands.' (2 Tim. 1:6) He also urged Timothy to study the Word of God as 'a worker' (2:15), and to 'keep a close watch on yourself and on the teaching … for by so doing you will save both yourself and your hearers' (1 Tim. 4:16).

The mandate is unmistakable. Leaders must continually seek to develop themselves by God's grace, and that requires personal discipline – the discipline of grace. Notice I did not say discipline *for* grace, but the discipline *of* grace. How? By living a lifestyle in which you daily 'put off your old self' and 'put on the new self' (Eph. 4:22-24). In your own power, this task is impossible. But you don't have to do it alone. God provides the means of grace through which His Spirit and His Word will work in your life, for your good and His glory, and will give you the ability to employ them. Remember this is not self-discipline to earn grace because our discipline is the result of grace as a gracious work from God (Phil. 2:12-13).

God's Word provides for us one case of perfect personal development, and obviously that is Jesus. There is a verse that describes His personal formation: 'Jesus increased in wisdom and in stature and in favor with God and man.' (Luke 2:52) Have you ever thought about the model presented to us there? Christ is not only our Redeemer but also our ultimate example, and in that verse we are provided a simple yet profound paradigm for personal formation. How did our Lord, in His humanity, grow and develop into a great leader? The biblical answer is *in wisdom* (intellectual formation), *in stature* (physical formation), *in favor with God* (spiritual formation), and *in favor with man* (relational formation). The Word of God has provided for us a biblically-defined plan that is far wiser than anything that human ingenuity could produce, and our Savior has given us the power by His transforming grace to enact it even as He Himself is the perfect model for us to imitate.

'Wisdom' – Intellectual Formation

Divine wisdom is necessary for a leader to make decisions that honor the Lord. Proverbs 9:10 reveals that 'the fear of the Lord is the beginning of wisdom'. So, what does that mean? It means that we must know who God is, what our relationship is with Him, and for what purpose He has called us. The God who loves us is truly awesome, and we are directed to love Him in return with both intimacy and reverence. His majesty and holiness make it all the more extraordinary that He loves us enough to mount a cross so that we might know Him savingly, follow Him obediently, and serve Him faithfully forever. Wisdom begins with and leads us to this kind of understanding about who God is and who we are to be by His grace and for His glory.

Scripture also teaches that biblical wisdom is ultimately demonstrated in our behavior. 'By his good conduct,' declares James 3:13, 'let him show his works in the meekness of wisdom'; and according to James 3:17, 'wisdom from above is first pure, then peaceable, gentle, open to reason, full of mercy and good fruits, impartial and sincere.' In these passages James is echoing the primary theme of the book of Proverbs by telling us that we should seek knowledge, understanding, and wisdom. It is not enough to merely have knowledge – it must be embraced with understanding. And true knowledge and understanding will lead to wisdom, which is manifested in the transformed life James describes.

Nowhere in Scripture does God tell us to be 'smart', nor does it ever promote mere intelligence. That highly valued human commodity is obviously not extolled by the Creator of the universe in isolation from understanding and wisdom. God wants us to have wisdom – His wisdom – from above, which begins with acknowledging that our loving Father is the God of the ages and committing to live in a manner that honors Him, while seeking to obey His Word in all areas of our life. We do that by learning the

Word and applying it thoughtfully to our lives. This is the most sure evidence of a new heart, which will always be a surrendered and yielding one (Ezek. 11:19; 36:26).

> The Word of God has provided for us a biblically-defined plan of leadership development that is far wiser than anything that human ingenuity could produce, and our Savior has given us the power by His transforming grace to enact it, even as He Himself is the perfect model for us to imitate.

'Stature' – Physical Formation

The human body is 'a temple of the Holy Spirit' (1 Cor. 6:19), and the Word commands each of us to 'present your bodies as a living sacrifice' (Rom. 12:1). Having a surrendered heart leads us to pursue obedience to these scriptural directives: God's people should strive to live with a regimen of rest, exercise, and diet that honors God. Another passage drives that point home: 'So, whether you eat or drink, or whatever you do, do all to the glory of God.' (1 Cor. 10:31) Christians should not live to eat and drink, which is idolatry, but instead should eat and drink to live for Christ, which is true worship.

We should also be obedient and responsible in getting our daily rest, and we should observe the Sabbath commandment for weekly rest and worship: 'Six days you shall labor, and do all your work, but the seventh day is a Sabbath to the LORD your God.' (Exod. 20:9-10) The Lord's Day is God's gift to man, according to Jesus: 'The Sabbath was made for man, not man for the Sabbath.' (Mark 2:27) When Jesus took the disciples away to pray, they kept falling asleep. His response and analysis were both insightful and pastoral: 'The spirit indeed is willing, but the flesh is weak.' (Matt. 26:41) In other words, Jesus knew that in their hearts and souls they desired to pray with Him, but physically they were neither ready for nor used to periods of extended prayer.

Paul wrote: 'I discipline my body and keep it under control [or 'make it my slave'].' (1 Cor. 9:27) Why? Because he knew that his ministry was demanding and the challenges daunting.

He wanted his body ready for those challenges. The success of physical discipline usually depends upon the vitality of spiritual discipline – the fruit of the Spirit passage concludes by affirming the promised blessing of 'self-control' (Gal. 5:22). But the physical disciplines also affect our spiritual lives. If we stay up late on Saturday night, for example, we likely will not be able to worship the Lord with spiritual vitality on Sunday morning. As one preacher said, '*Saturday Night Live* is Sunday morning dead.' Your body is not a container that carries your spirit and soul. Your body is like a thread, and your spirit and soul is another thread. These two threads are woven into one cloth, which is your life. What you do with one inevitably will affect the other. Grace-enabled spiritual growth will encourage physical discipline, and physical discipline positions you for greater spiritual growth.

'Favor with God' – Spiritual Formation

Luke 2:52 says that Jesus also grew 'in favor with God'. Since this part of our development is so important and foundational, let us take some extra time to consider some barriers and aids to spiritual formation.

Barriers to spiritual formation

What are the barriers, obstacles, and pitfalls which prevent and challenge our spiritual formation in Christ and for Christ? Here are some reasons:

An inability to say 'No.' As Christians, we're called to live a simple life. Paul in 1 Thessalonians 4:11 advises us to 'aspire to live quietly, and to mind your own affairs'. Simplicity in life requires being willing and able to say 'no'. Most Christians are too busy. We have allowed the world to set our life's schedule, resulting in ineffective busyness. We have lost the ability to prioritize in general, and we have very little understanding of biblical priorities in particular.

In Luke 10, our Lord was enjoying the hospitality of two sisters, Martha and Mary. Mary was sitting 'at the Lord's feet' listening to His teaching. In contrast, Martha 'was distracted with much serving'. The latter sister then complained to the Lord: 'Do you not care that my sister has left me to serve alone? Tell her then to help me.' The Lord's answer was instructive and challenging: 'Martha, Martha. You are anxious and troubled about many things but one thing is necessary. Mary has chosen the good portion which will not be taken away from her.' (Luke 10:38-42) Today this is called FOMO – Fear of Missing Out. People are insatiably searching for meaningful experiences so they try to do anything and everything which is marketed as something that will make your life meaningful.

There was nothing wrong with Martha's commitment to serve. But our Lord was affirming Mary's commitment to elevate the priority of hearing God's Word and then intentionally implementing that priority in her life, which meant she had to say 'no' to some things in order to 'yes' to the right things.

Effective serving in life is dependent upon prioritizing time with the Lord in His Word, and Mary had 'chosen the good portion'. Out of that she would be able to serve, but serving should never trump the hearing of God's Word. Mary was spending her time doing something even more worthwhile than hospitality and service.

But the fact is, you can't and won't say 'no' until you have a bigger 'yes'. To have a bigger 'yes', you have to know God's priorities from His Word, which also instructs you in the principles needed to make wise decisions. Establishing and maintaining biblical priorities and properly ordering our lives is not easy for Christian leaders. We love people and want to serve them – plus there is an ever-subtle tendency to think that busyness will convince others of our value.

Find God's 'yesses' from His Word. A biblical 'yes' will be big enough for you to say 'no' appropriately and kindly, but firmly and at the right time.

Shortchanging your time alone with the Lord. Examine the lifestyle of a ministry leader who has failed, and you will frequently find a lack of personal time with the Lord. Often, even among mature ministers, the first thing sacrificed to an overly demanding lifestyle is their time alone with God. If you are not experiencing a daily relationship with the Lord, you are much more likely to stumble or fall. You need times of silence, reflection, and renewal. Psalm 62:1 says it perfectly: 'For God alone my soul waits in silence.'

Church leaders can often neglect time alone with the Lord because they are frequently worshiping and praying with others, and they think that is sufficient. But imagine a marriage where the wife never spends any time alone with her husband, because she says they're 'together all the time' when they're with others. Just like that marriage will not be healthy until the couple plans some 'alone time', so we as the bride of Christ should make it a priority to spend time alone with our beloved Savior.

Living beyond your means. Advertising agencies are committed to making yesterday's luxuries today's necessities, and they are extremely effective in their marketing schemes. Too many Christians in today's materialistic world, including leaders, find themselves with 'too much month at the end of the money' because they have bought into a conspicuous consumer lifestyle.

How do you avoid the materialistic traps in today's culture? Here's a simple plan: First repent from any covetousness in your heart, then write down the income that God has given you. Subtract your tithe, and then the offerings that you are led to give beyond the tithe. Then arrange a lifestyle that works with what's left. Adopt a lifestyle within your means, and don't automatically expand it when your income increases. While debt is not sin, you can be sinfully in debt. Conspicuous consumerism is driven by having to get the next thing with an eye-catching label, believing that this is the key to a meaningful life. Actually it is a form of idolatry that will bring God's discipline.

Just like a marriage will not be healthy until the couple plans some 'alone time', so we as the bride of Christ should make it a priority to spend time alone with our beloved Savior.

Our Lord will give us what we need, and if He gives us more resources than we need, it is likely for the purpose of expanding our ministry capacity. How much you have does not really concern the Lord. What does concern Him is, does what you have actually have you? Matthew 6:33 tells us to 'seek first the kingdom of God and His righteousness, and all these things will be added to you.' Too many of us seek things first and allow the Lord to be a mere addition. But life is not about things; 'to live is Christ'. Things are not our life. 'For what does it profit a man to gain the whole world and forfeit his soul?' (Mark 8:36) Do not let things use you and draw you away from Him who loves you and has loosed you from your sins (Rev. 1:5).

Forfeiting the opportunity to give sacrificially. What a blessing it is to give sacrificially of our time, energy, and money. When we learn to live within our means and spend our time wisely by living with simplicity, we establish margins from which we are then able to respond to opportunities of ministry and to give sacrificially.

Don't forfeit those God-given opportunities with a careless or materialistic lifestyle. If you live within your means – willing to go without when you can and managing finances responsibly – you can give sacrificially when God presents a need. Living a disciplined lifestyle will allow you to have the ability to give of your time, energy, and money because your simplicity will have created an abundance in your life. Do that, and you will be repeatedly reminded that it really is 'more blessed to give than to receive' (Acts 20:35).

Neglecting to fast – with prayer and the Word. Are you reluctant to fast? Do you associate it with hunger strikes and grim-faced self-denial? Or with boastful adherents who proudly (and unbiblically) announce that they are fasting? Well, forget those notions. They are parodies of genuine fasting, which can be a blessing in many ways. It is not self-inflicted punishment; it is devotion – and you should not neglect it. It is simply a joyful exercise of setting aside something you don't need in exchange for a calculated focus on the Lord. Fasting should always be accompanied by prayer and the Word, so skip lunch once in a while and spend that time with Him. Set aside your hobby occasionally and give that time to the Lord. Devote a break time to Scripture instead of Starbucks. Set aside a day and spend it in devotional Bible reading, prayer, meditation, and time to be alone with God. What a joy that will be for you!

Keep it to yourself – the biblical admonition in Matthew 6:16-18 is to tell nobody but the Lord that you are fasting. Then enjoy the blessings that result from a special moment of intimacy with the God who loves you.

Succumbing to sexual sin. It is so obviously wrong and horribly harmful – yet it is so incredibly common. Outright adultery is painfully common in ministry leadership, and pornography is even more pervasive. Do not succumb to it! Remember the biblical fall of King David, which began with idleness, roving eyes, and a lustful heart, then descended to adultery and murder. Stop the downfall when it's a spark, not a flame – and certainly before it's a wildfire.

In other words, don't resist temptation, 'flee it'. Sometimes we mix up biblical principles in life decisions. For instance, we exalt ourselves and then pray for humility when the Bible says 'humble yourselves and He will exalt you at the right time'. Another one is that we 'flee Satan' and resist temptation but actually the Bible says, 'resist Satan and he will flee from you' and 'flee temptation'. Do not trust in your own strength to resist. Instead, flee temptation and fill your heart with a love for Christ and your spouse. When a heart is filled with Godly love there is no room for the obsessions of sexual idolatry. Ask the Lord to give you a revulsion to even the thought of sexual immorality and an obsession with the joy of the marriage bed, which is holy. Then find friends of the same gender who will love you enough to pray for you and hold you accountable while encouraging you to 'fix your eyes on Jesus'. Remember that a saved sinner is still a sinner, and never put yourself in harm's way. Never. And never rely on your own strength: 'Put no confidence in the flesh' (Phil. 3:3), while always depending wholly upon the grace of God in Christ.

Aids to spiritual formation

When we are working hard to eliminate those barriers, we are ready to grow spiritually. Our new life in Christ is vibrant and vital, but it must always be regularly and abundantly nourished. Historically we have called these biblically-ordained practices of personal spiritual nourishment 'the means of grace'. They enable you to strengthen and deepen the intimacy of your relationship with the Lord. Let's examine them.

Personal prayer life. In Matthew 6:6, the Lord instructs us to find a time and a place where we can privately come to Him in prayer. We endanger our spiritual health when we neglect having a quiet time, but we receive great blessings when we make it a priority. The demands on leaders may be greater than on other believers, but their need for a consistent quiet time is even greater. All children need some alone time with their father, and you do, too – with your heavenly Father.

Personal Bible study. Prayer and the Word should be inseparable. Christian leaders need systematic, focused time in the Word of God. It's that simple. And that vital. Perhaps this practice that has helped me will also help you: Set aside a sacred place and time that you meet the Lord each day to be nourished in Him through His Word and prayer. Mine is in the morning, so the night before, I go to the appointed place where I will meet the Lord the next morning and place my Bible, my journal, and my other devotional material there. Have you noticed that when someone sets the table, we always seem to make it to the table to be fed and nourished? So set the spiritual table the night before. It will help you in the discipline of arriving there with expectation the next day.

> Matthew 6:33 tells us to 'seek first the kingdom of God and His righteousness, and all these things will be added to you.' Too many of us seek things first and allow the Lord to be a mere addition.

Memorization and meditation. When encountering the Lord through personal Bible study and being drawn close to Him in personal prayer, every believer has the opportunity to enhance that experience through memorization of and meditation on the Word of God. Sadly, contemporary American culture is so adrift that many people equate meditation with Eastern mysticism. How far we have strayed! Transcendental meditation – grievously popular even in our churches today – is the emptying of the mind for the purpose of self-absorption. In contrast, meditation on the Word of God is the intentional filling of heart and mind with God's revealed truth, illuminated by His Holy Spirit.

Meditating on the Word inspires us, comforts us, directs us, and protects us spiritually, as noted in Psalm 119:11: 'I have stored up your word in my heart, that I might not sin against you.' Memorization enables us to always be prepared to meditate on God's Word in any circumstance of life, and meditation leads us to reflection – applying the Word to our personal situation. It's a glorious and essential exercise in a believer's personal relationship with Jesus Christ and will usually lead to the recognition of our sins, and how we have 'fallen short of the glory of God' (Rom. 3:23). This leads us to our next discipline.

Confession. Through reflection on the Word, the Holy Spirit convicts us of our sins. Remember, Satan wants to condemn us, to make us feel worthless, and to pull us down and away from God. That is condemnation, which Satan wants to use to discourage us as God's ambassadors. In contrast, true Holy Spirit conviction prompts us to confess our sins and repent with full assurance that God will forgive us and 'renew a right spirit within [us]' (Ps. 51:10). That is God's way of drawing us back to Him in order for us to know His love.

Satan condemns and neutralizes; God convicts and inspires. So keep 'short accounts' with God by being always ready to confess sin when He convicts you. Remember, we are promised that 'If we confess our sins, he is faithful and just to forgive us our sins and to cleanse us from all unrighteousness' (1 John 1:9).

Consecration. Forgiveness is granted to believers once and for all time through God's grace by the finished work of Jesus Christ on the cross. As we build our relationship with Him through prayer, the Word, meditating, reflecting, and confessing sin, we experience the ongoing joy of our salvation. By God's grace we are refreshed, renewed, and empowered to consecrate ourselves to His service. To *consecrate* means to 'set apart or dedicate', and Bible-based leadership should be exercising every means of grace to do that in an ever-growing lifestyle of intimacy with the Lord.

The lyrics of the old hymn 'Just as I Am, Thine Own to Be' have it right: 'To consecrate myself to Thee, O Jesus Christ, I come…'

'Favor with Man' – Relational Formation

As we confront the culture around us, believers in general and Christian leaders in particular must do so with the love of Christ. The model that the Lord gives us in Luke 2:52 calls us to grow in favor with 'man', or the people of this world, both saved and lost.

Those who are not believers should see Jesus in us. We should be different. One noticeable difference should be a loving, caring heart. Our relationships with nonbelievers should be genuine, loving, and respectful. That will open the door for effective evangelism. Other believers should see Christ in us too, and be encouraged by that same loving, Christ-filled heart. Exhibiting the love of Christ should be the goal of every believer – and it is absolutely essential to effective Christian leadership.

Do you want to model Christ as a leader? Embrace the love of Christ: sacrificial, humble, selfless love. Again, you cannot do it by yourself – nobody can – but by God's grace and empowered by His Holy Spirit, you can indeed radiate the love of Christ. What a witness that will be to the lost, and what an encouragement to the saved.

An old adage (which my wife has framed in needlepoint in our home) makes a powerful point: 'The greatest thing a father can do for his children is to love their mother.' How true that is, and how influential is the love of a husband toward a wife. Even more powerful, however, is the love of Christ shown to others through us. This ought to be like needlepoint on the heart of every Christian leader: 'The greatest thing a child of God can do for his Father is to show the Father's love to others.'

As a leader, you must remember that all of our relationships with others are affected by our relationship with the Lord. If you want to be a leader who models Christ, who increases in favor with man, you must be serious about increasing in your knowledge of the favor of God provided for you in Christ. Our intimate relationship with Him must increasingly be genuine, vibrant, and vigorous. The result of being intimate with Christ will be demonstrated by the love of Christ permeating our human relationships. In John 13:35, all believers – leaders included – are at once both admonished and encouraged by the Lord: 'By this all people will know that you are my disciples, if you have love for one another.'

Before *going* as a leader, you must be *growing* in the Lord. So grow,

in wisdom.

in stature.

in favor with God.

and in favor with man.

That is what each individual can do to prepare to be an effective leader in Christ's church; and in society as well. In the next chapter, we will look into what the church as a whole can do to encourage this kind of Christ-like growth in its members.

Questions for Thought and Discussion

1) What are some ways that the life and ministry of Jesus, as recorded in the Gospels, show that He had grown in wisdom when He was younger? How about in stature? In favor with God? In favor with man?

2) What are some differences between Godly wisdom and mere intellectual knowledge?

3) What are some examples of how your spiritual life has affected you physically, and vice versa?

4) What were some barriers and aids to spiritual formation and growth in the lives of some well-known Bible characters? Consider, for example: Moses, Sarah, David, Esther, and Peter.

5) Think more about the relationship between your ministry to others and the other aspects of spiritual growth discussed in this chapter. How does your 'favor with man' depend upon the other three? Pray that by God's grace you will 'practice these things, immerse yourself in them, so that all may see your progress' (1 Tim. 4:15)

Chapter 7

The Church as a Leadership Factory

H E'S alive!

The news raced through Jerusalem that Jesus of Nazareth – crucified, dead, and buried – was now alive, and eyewitnesses had verified the reports. He had risen from the dead, appeared to more than five hundred of His followers, and ascended to heaven amidst a cloud of glory.

Already Jesus – Y'shua, Messiah, the Christ – was causing an even greater impact through His death, resurrection, and ascension than He did in life. Thousands were coming to faith in Him, and the historical narrative of this kingdom movement of the Gospel is found in the book of Acts. The second chapter describes the lifestyle of these new believers – how they loved to hear God's Word, worshiped, prayed, and gave to those in need.

But to sustain this amazing movement into future generations and change the world permanently, they would have to multiply leaders.

Multiplication in the Early Church

The book of Acts also records how the Apostles, whom Christ had trained, produced an amazing proliferation of leaders.

One of the converts – Joseph of Cyprus – became so well known for his sacrificial life and gift of encouragement that his name was changed (Acts 4:36). Instead of calling him Joseph, the believers came to call him *Barnabas* – *Bar* meaning 'son of' and *nabas* meaning 'encouragement'. The old Joseph became the new 'son of encouragement' because the grace of God had given him a new heart and new life, and he became a key leader in the early church.

Another dramatic conversion came to a religious terrorist named Saul, who had persecuted, imprisoned, and killed Christians in the mistaken notion that he was serving God. After his conversion he was initially shunned by the Apostles because they feared and mistrusted him, but Barnabas defended Saul and personally discipled him. A few years later, after God had blessed Barnabas with a ministry beyond his capacity in Antioch, he sent for Saul, whom he had helped develop as a leader, preacher, and teacher. Directed by the Holy Spirit, the church at Antioch dispatched Barnabas and Saul on a mission trip, which has become known as the 'first missionary journey'.

Since Scripture speaks of them as 'Barnabas and Saul', the order of their names indicates that Saul was still under the tutelage of Barnabas. Yet by the time they returned, Saul also had undergone a name change. He had become *Paul*, which means 'small' in Greek and fits well with his humble description of himself as 'the least of the Apostles'. Interestingly and informatively, by the end of the first missionary journey, the name order had also shifted. Instead of 'Barnabas and Saul,' it had become 'Paul and Barnabas'.

The Apostles who had been trained by Christ multiplied themselves, and Barnabas, one of the new leaders, followed their example by developing Paul as a leader. He was so effective and successful as a trainer that Paul eventually became *his* leader.

Someone who performs in a large symphony once told me that the hardest position to fill in the orchestra is second-chair violinist. No one wants to play 'second fiddle'. But if Barnabas struggled with the sin of pride, he conquered it in Christ because he developed leaders so successfully that they even went beyond him in ministry effectiveness. He moved willingly from the premier position in ministry to the new status of 'second fiddle' – apparently mindful of the biblical admonition that 'the last shall be first'.

Acts 15 says that Paul suggested taking a second missionary journey with Barnabas. Although Barnabas initially felt led to go, he wanted to make his cousin John Mark part of the missionary team. Paul rejected the idea because he thought that Mark might quit along the way, as he had on the first missionary journey. But Barnabas wanted to give Mark another chance – remember he is the 'son of encouragement' – because he saw the young man's potential as a leader. Paul disagreed sharply because he was developing a team of proven leaders, not potential leaders for the specific task at hand. The result was that Mark went on a separate mission trip with Barnabas, while Paul took Silas on his, so both Mark and Silas ended up being trained further by these 'multiplication leaders'.

Interestingly, Mark was subsequently and consequentially well-equipped, and he matured as a leader under Barnabas and later became the author of a Gospel as a crucial member of Peter's ministry team. Peter acknowledged Mark's maturity and his close relationship with him in 1 Peter 5:13, referring to Mark as 'my son'. Paul also acknowledged Mark's growth from a potential leader to a proven leader in Colossians 4:10, where he says: 'Aristarchus my fellow prisoner greets you, and Mark the cousin of Barnabas (concerning whom you have received instructions – if he comes to you, welcome him).' Furthermore, at the end of his life, Paul demonstrated his respect for Mark by saying he was 'very useful to me for ministry' (2 Tim. 4:11).

The Jesus Model of Multiplication

How did the early church develop so many leaders so effectively? Inspired by the Holy Spirit, in his final letter to Timothy, Paul outlined the biblical concept of multiplication leadership at the end of his life: 'You then, my child, be strengthened by the grace that is in Christ Jesus, and what you have heard from me in the presence of many witnesses entrust to faithful men who will be able to teach others also.' (2 Tim. 2:1-2)

This passage clearly sets forth the '3D' approach to leadership multiplication, as it implies that leaders must be *defined*, *developed*, and *deployed*. The Lord had previously demonstrated the same approach in His three-year-long earthly ministry. In this 'Jesus Model' – which was followed by Barnabas, Paul, and other

New Testament leaders – a principal leader multiplies himself, developing proven leaders from potential leaders, who then attract other potential leaders.

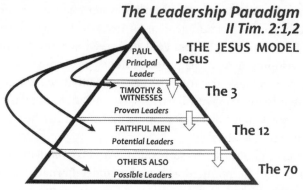

The biblical model of leadership multiplication that is so clearly delineated in 2 Timothy 2:1-2 called Timothy to imitate Paul just as Paul imitated Christ. Paul was the *principal* leader. He invested himself in Timothy, who was the *proven* leader, according to Philippians 2:22: 'But you know Timothy's proven worth, how as a son with a father he has served with me in the Gospel.' Other proven leaders were apparently learning along with Timothy, according to 2 Timothy 2:1-2, to whom Paul refers with the statement: 'what you have heard from me in the presence of many witnesses.' Some of these other proven leaders were Aquila and Priscilla, Silas, Titus, and Luke. As *proven* leaders, Timothy and the others then helped to develop *potential* leaders, who are profiled as 'faithful men who will be able to teach others also'.

Applying the Model Today

Notice the two distinctive marks of *potential* leaders in 2 Timothy 2:2.

First, *potential* leaders should be consistent enough in their spiritual lives to be called 'faithful'. Secondly, they should be willing to multiply by conducting their ministry through a team of other *possible* leaders, who are called 'others' in the text. Here Paul is affirming, like Jesus before him, that the church's ministry is best done through teams. The *principal* leader is the pastor, who should invest in a team of *proven* leaders (i.e., ordained officers and staff), who each conduct ministry through teams of *potential* leaders ('faithful men'), and then develop ministry teams of *possible* leaders ('others'). So ministry through teams of leaders must be a non-negotiable commitment in any church or ministry. Every leader should be on a team and do ministry through a team of leaders, each of whom also lead ministry teams themselves.

When ministry is carried out through teams of leaders, extraordinary benefits and blessings accrue. For instance, when more proven leaders are needed, team ministry will have developed them through training and experience. Likewise, other potential leaders will continually surface through ministry endeavors. Team ministry also provides nurture, accountability, and encouragement, as well as multiple insights and sources of wisdom. In the church 3D Leadership – *defining, developing*, and *deploying* leaders – depends greatly on a pastor who delights in training new leaders and sharing leadership through an intentional commitment to doing ministry through teams of leaders.

Under the Lord, the pastor as the *principal* leader must first develop a team of *proven* leaders who are committed to further the ministry by developing *potential* leaders, each of whom can commit to conducting ministry with a team of other potential leaders. Leadership formation thus occurs throughout the entire ministry infrastructure just as it did in the New Testament church. As a result the church can again become a leadership factory and distribution center that will impact families, communities, and the entire culture.

How can the pastor of a local church implement the principle of team ministry that multiplies leadership? Here are some suggestions:

- Teach the biblical principle of leadership multiplication and mobilization from 2 Timothy 2:1-2.

- Establish a non-negotiable precedent of conducting ministry through teams of leaders, and declare that every leader is to be on a team and every leader must do their ministry through a team.

- Recruit a team of *proven* leaders, each of whom will commit to recruiting a team of *potential* leaders, each of whom in turn will commit to recruiting 'others' – *possible* leaders.

- Apply the biblical principle of leadership through teams to all areas of ministry in the church.

- Obtain a commitment from the formal church leaders that ministry will always be performed in teams and that the goal of each team will include developing leaders as well as achieving ministry.

- Take the lead in communicating the pivotal point that existing leadership should always develop 'teams of leaders' rather than 'leadership teams'. 'Leadership teams' tend to become the servants of the team leader. But if you develop 'teams of leaders', the team leader will have to become a servant to those leaders on the team in order to promote their success by becoming a leader of leaders, rather than being supported as a leader by a leadership team of followers.

In this biblical paradigm of leadership development, new leaders inevitably 'bubble up' from the inside. This ministry infrastructure of teams of leaders will generate leaders internally, who have been discipled by knowledgeable Christian leaders instead of depending upon recruiting leaders from outside who have been discipled by the world. Then the church will be a leadership factory not only for the church itself but also for the family and every sphere of society, including business, the arts, and government. And of course, it will not stop here in America – praise the Lord – but will even be used to send the Gospel to all the other nations of the world.

From Leadership Teams to a Team of Leaders

It is not God's plan for any leader to be a Lone Ranger. It takes teamwork, and a carefully and prayerfully selected team of leaders is essential. It's the biblical model of leadership, and it works for leadership multiplication and mobilization. A *principal* leader defines, develops, and deploys *proven* leaders, who develop *potential* leaders, who in turn develop *possible* leaders. So let's learn more about how to create teams of leaders, and make them work in the best way possible.

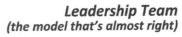

Leadership Team
(the model that's almost right)

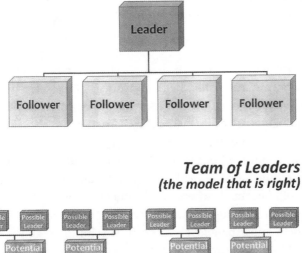

Team of Leaders
(the model that is right)

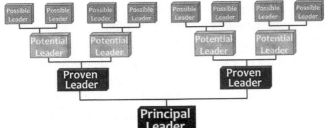

Choosing the team members

Recruiting a team of leaders requires prayer, care, and wisdom.

The obvious first step is to establish criteria for identifying leaders for the team. Let's call those criteria the 'Six Cs' – calling, character, content, competency, commitment, and chemistry. In Chapter 5 we talked about three of them – character, content, and competency – when considering the traits we want to develop in leaders. Here we will be discussing how those traits, and some others, need to be present to some growing degree in people before we select them for a team of leaders.

Calling. Leaders must have a calling. They should have prayerfully evaluated their desire and willingness to serve in ministry – they want to be leaders for the right reasons and be willing to pay the price of leadership out of love for the Lord. They should understand that while salvation is free, discipleship will cost, and leadership will cost even more. Furthermore, they should be recognized as leaders by others. They should have surrendered to God's internal calling to leadership and have external confirmation of that calling through evaluation, affirmation, and recognition by others.

Character. As we've said before, character is an absolutely essential key to leadership. Before anyone is granted the privilege of occupying the position of leader, his or her personal character and conduct must be affirmed. Every Christian has a spiritual gift for ministry, and every Christian is fully saved from all of his or her sins, yet not everyone is qualified to be a leader. Those who are called to leadership are held to a higher standard: 'Not many of you should become teachers, my brothers, for you know that we who teach will be judged with greater strictness.' (James 3:1)

Leaders 'must be above reproach' (1 Tim. 3:2), and it is the responsibility of church overseers to ensure that leaders possess consistent character before they are deployed. Not only must a leader be qualified, but a leader can also be disqualified through careless conduct and sinful lifestyle decisions. Remember, leadership is a privilege, not a right that you have simply because you are a Christian. It is bestowed by recognition of your calling and consistent progress in the grace of God as a follower of Christ.

Content. Leaders should 'know their stuff'. First, they should be rooted and grounded in the Word of God and should know what it means to be a follower of Christ with a loving commitment to biblical integrity. Next, they should know their stuff when it comes to principled Christian leadership in their specific area of expertise. If they lead a worship team, they should know worship. If they lead an administrative team, they should know administration. If they lead an outreach team, they should know evangelism. In whatever ministry to which they are called, they also should know how to reproduce and multiply themselves through their own ministry team of leaders. But remember, most of all, they must know the Word of God to a growing degree so they can share it with those they are going to lead.

Competency. Calling, character, and content are utilized for God's glory through leadership competencies. Proven leaders not only should 'know their stuff' but must also be competent in the skills required to accomplish their ministry for the Lord. Specifically, they should have acquired the skills necessary to accomplish their particular mission and ministry. Moreover, they should continue to improve those skills and acquire others as needed. Not only is competency necessary for the efficient exercise of leadership, but it also simultaneously encourages and provides comfort to those who are in the care of a leader. They are confident that he or she not only knows what to do but by God's grace is able to competently achieve it.

Commitment. Just as Paul advised Timothy to 'fulfill' the ministry to which he had been called (2 Tim. 4:5), modern leaders also need unwavering commitment. The objective of a leader is not self-fulfillment but self-sacrifice to achieve ministry fulfillment. Ironically, however, that is also the only real path to personal fulfillment. To be 'poured out as a drink offering', as Paul said about his ministry in 2 Timothy 4:6, may be all-consuming, but it is also exceedingly satisfying in the end.

Chemistry. Finally, leaders must learn how to work as a team, which requires relational chemistry. This is one of the greatest challenges facing a leader when building a team of leaders. In the hands of a competent and committed scientist, combining elements to achieve a necessary compound is not a mystery. But leadership chemistry is much more of an art than a science. Therefore, I suggest that whenever a team of leaders is being assembled, these three questions should be asked and answered in the affirmative before moving ahead:

- Does each team member comprehend and embrace the ministry vision and its goals?

- Does each team member recognize and personally commit to support the principal leader?

- Will each team member commit to developing and sustaining meaningful and supportive relationships with others on the team?

If you are placed in the position of interviewing a leadership candidate, never give in to the temptation to manipulate an affirmative answer to any of the above questions. Never go unprepared into an interview with a leadership candidate. Always be responsible to the ministry and the candidate by thoroughly examining every reference and securing secondary references. When interviewing a leadership candidate, be pleasant, of course, but be serious – not casual or informal. Being on a team of Christian leaders is never a frivolous issue. Don't downplay the costs of leadership. Don't do a 'soft sell' or 'bait and switch', but instead provide accurate information about the ministry and a frank assessment of the responsibilities and challenges, as well as the opportunities.

It is also essential to allow the candidate time for prayer and reflection before accepting a position on the team of leaders. So even if these questions are answered affirmatively, avoid pushing the candidate to immediately accept the position offered. A follow-up interview is usually prudent.

When all of the members of the team sincerely affirm those questions, you have made a good start and are well on your way to the chemistry that the team will need.

Prayer, counsel, and change

Authentic *calling*, consistent *character*, sufficient *content*, demonstrated *competency*, heartfelt *commitment*, and productive *chemistry* provide a strong foundation for any team's ministry, if empowered by the Holy Spirit. But prayer is required for those qualifications to be truly present, and for that power to be at work in the team. Remember, a Christian leader should not only pray for the work of the ministry but also realize that prayer *is* the work of the ministry. Nothing else we do is more important than intercessory prayer for leaders and leadership. Develop a team of leaders that makes prayer a priority. Prayer must precede the selection of leadership, permeate the work of leadership, and promote the effects of that work afterwards. We have not because we ask not (James 4:2).

And do not fail to seek the insights of wise counselors. Proverbs 15:22 says, 'Without counsel plans fail, but with many advisers they succeed.' The specific quantity of advisers may be relative – two may be 'many' in some situations; several or more may be 'many' in others. But Scripture repeatedly emphasizes the quality of counsel: it must be 'wise' (Prov. 20:18; 24:6). Wise counsel is biblical counsel, and biblical counsel flows most readily from those who are walking with the Lord faithfully and consistently. Seek advice from such spiritually mature people and listen to their counsel, always testing everything by the Word of God (Acts 17:11).

One issue that will require much prayer and counsel is possible changes of personnel in a team. When is such a change appropriate? And if it is appropriate, how do you implement it? The brief answer is that you always make changes by following biblical precepts and guidelines. If a team of leaders is unable to achieve the mission, then either the mission is wrong and needs to be reconsidered, or the right team is not in place and needs to be re-formed. It's possible that both may be true, but usually it is one or the other.

The team mission may need to be re-examined to make sure that everything is biblical, God-centered, and strategically appropriate. Has the ministry become man-centered or man-dependent? If so, there is not only a need to refocus and re-form, but also to repent. 'Seek first the kingdom of God and His righteousness,' Matthew 6:33 promises us, 'and all these things will be added to you.'

If you are the *principal* leader, you should first prayerfully examine yourself before the Lord. Have you contributed to the lack of success? If so, you should assume responsibility, make changes, or even resign. If the problem is the composition of the team, does a personnel change need to be made? Whenever I am praying about a change of personnel on a team of leaders, I always ask myself two questions about the individual under consideration to determine if I am on the right track: (1) If that individual resigned, would I be glad? If so, either my heart is not right toward that team member or that person should probably not be on the team. (2) If that position were vacant, would I fill it with the individual who currently occupies it? If not – and my heart is right – then that person should probably not be on the team in that position.

If a change really is needed, how do you, as the principal leader of the team, bring it about? First, rather than focusing on removing someone, you should focus on helping the individual in question find where God wants him or her to be. Your first effort is to assist him or her in finding a right fit for his or her leadership abilities, style, and passion. You don't fix blame; you fix the problem. Often that means applying gifts and talents where they really belong. In other words, find the right team that fits people's leadership abilities. But, be careful: don't try to invent a job that fits the individual – that is usually a poor short-term solution and causes other problems later.

Sometimes when personnel changes are needed on the team, personal confession and repentance are required, as well as reciprocal forgiveness. The team of leaders will not experience God's full blessing if serious issues are ignored and sin is covered instead of confessed. If, after prayer and wise counsel, the team member in question still resists the change, or if the change produces bitterness and resentment that affect the team, the entire team may need to become involved. Any conflict in a church ministry should be resolved biblically by the church leadership authority. In a parachurch ministry, such resolution is usually the responsibility of the ministry's oversight board.

Of course, the key text that guides resolution and reconciliation for all Christians, including Christian leaders, is Matthew 18:15-18. If outside counsel or conciliation is required, I recommend seeking help from Peacemaker Ministries (www.peacemaker.net), which offers guidance in biblical conflict resolution and in proactively creating a culture of peace in an organization.

Making a team of leaders work well

So now you have a team of leaders. How can you enhance the team's performance? How can you elevate the energy and motivation of the team?

First, remember that teams are like people – their energy level rises and falls for a variety of reasons during the seasons of life. Just as our individual bodies need rest, nourishment, and exercise in order to be energized, so leadership teams need sources of energy. The following are five energy sources that elevate a team's ability to perform with vitality.

Embrace the team leader and the concept of teams. The team leader brings passion, excitement, and energy for the team vision and mission, but only if he or she is embraced as the leader. If you are the leader, remember that your support is based on respect and trust. Titles identify the one who should be respected and trusted, but they do not create respect and trust. Your Gospel-driven life and effective leadership is what will elicit them – so regularly 'draw near to God, and he will draw near to you' (James 4:8).

Embrace the team vision and mission. It is exciting to see how a vision of genuine God-centered worship can become an energized reality when a worship team of leaders embraces their mission with passion, commitment, and humble hearts. Likewise, an outreach team of leaders that embraces its mission will be energized as it accomplishes the mission of planting churches and sending out missionaries. Evidence of spiritual maturity in the life of believers will inevitably energize small group disciple-making teams. And on it goes. When a team of leaders embraces the vision and mission, remembering that the vision and the mission must be biblical and thoughtfully contextualized, the team members will inevitably be motivated to do great things for God.

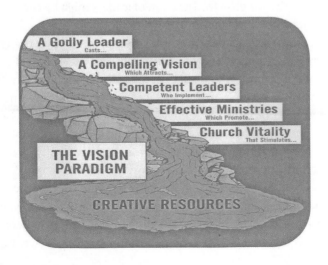

Embrace the members of the team of leaders. 'And let us consider how to stir up one another to love and good works, not neglecting to meet together, as is the habit of some, but encouraging one another, and all the more as you see the Day drawing near.' (Heb. 10:24-25) Team members bring energy to the mission through their interdependent relationships. Even team evaluations, instead of being a source of conflict, can be the catalyst for creating additional energy through the encouragement that comes from a balanced, biblically-based review and a mutual desire to stimulate each other to improvement.

If you're the *principal* leader, remember to maintain a servant's heart, but don't allow yourself to take over others' responsibilities. Do not do what the team can and should do for itself. The team of leaders must own the team leader, as he or she must own the vision and the mission, and its members must own and support each other. The principal leader should encourage that ownership and support, which will result in energizing both the team and the individual members as they affirm each other's strengths and assist each other in addressing the areas where there is needed improvement.

Embrace challenges as opportunities. If a team of leaders has bathed the mission and each other in prayer, then its members will be ready to respond to problems and obstacles as God-given opportunities for growth. The team of leaders must be encouraged to identify problems and obstacles, and not deny them.

That has been a personal weakness of mine – denying the presence of problems and obstacles. It is only recently that I have come to fully understand that challenges and problems are gifts from a Sovereign God, that when faced, solved, and overcome, will produce energy, cohesion, and a sense of accomplishment for the team. Team members actually become encouraged and motivated when they work together to solve problems. Ironically, problems can actually be an asset to team energy.

Football teams love to play on game day, and they love to score. But how do coaches keep football players focused and engaged during the long hours of practice? The mission is to score, to cross the goal line. So the coaches create a strategy to accomplish the mission and the players practice all week to implement that strategy, knowing that the other team will present eleven obstacles trying to stop them from scoring. A football team is energized in practice when it knows that it's preparing to remove those eleven obstacles through means like blocking, running, and passing. Without those obstacles there would be no motivation to work so hard in practice.

An effective team leader will encourage team members to accept obstacles and challenges as opportunities, and to seek the Lord's solutions. Good leaders neither deny the existence of problems nor let them become an excuse to quit. Make prayer a priority when difficulties arise. Lead the team members to jointly pursue solutions, and watch as their energetic engagement grows. As it grows, the team will also grow.

Celebrate the victories. Whenever God gives a victory, team leaders should pause to celebrate. Appropriate celebration honors the Lord who gave the victory and energizes the team of leaders. It is a mistake to move right on to the next effort without taking time to rejoice in what God has done.

In this chapter we have seen that the church can once again become a leadership factory and distribution center, and how it can achieve that goal through teams of leaders. But this all depends on the ability of leaders to multiply other leaders. In the next chapter (the concluding one for the dimension of *developing* leaders) we will learn more about how you, and those you raise up, can do that effectively.

Questions for Thought and Discussion

1) Review 2 Timothy 2:2, and memorize it as you do. How would you use that verse to explain the multiplication model of leadership to someone?

2) Think back to a time when you were selected to be a leader, or when you selected someone else for leadership. Were all the 'Six Cs' suggested in this chapter applied to that choice, and is there any way it could have been done better?

3) What are some problems that can occur in the 'chemistry' between members of a team? How could they be avoided?

4) Have you or anyone you know well ever been removed from a leadership position? Upon evaluating the process of removing the leader, what was done well and what could have been done better?

5) Review the 'energy sources' for teams at the end of the chapter, make a list of three ways you can apply them to your ministry, and pray about implementing them.

Chapter 8

Five Habits of Multiplication Leaders

IT is not about counting numbers but about the caliber of leaders. Many people think that effective leadership is measured by a large following. If that were true, we would have to respect some of the world's worst evils, such as communism and fascism, not to mention the billions of people who have been misled by counterfeit religions. Granted, lack of numerical growth *can* be an indication of something wrong somewhere. A large following, however, does not necessarily reflect the presence of biblical leadership. A truer test of an effective Bible-based leader lies not with the size of the followership, but with the quality of leaders he or she produces.

It is the quality of leaders, not the quantity of followers that matters. Effective biblical leadership normally produces multiplication and growth – the same way that rivulets become brooks, brooks become creeks, creeks become streams, and streams become mighty rivers. It is a process. Usually it requires the passage of time. Ministry movements sometimes take flight quickly, but usually the movements of God's kingdom arise as multiplication leaders are developed over a longer period of time.

When the biblical paradigm of leadership development is faithfully applied, leaders multiply, and as a consequence followers do as well. But remember, this process begins with genuine biblical leadership. For three years Christ *defined* leadership, *developed* leaders, and *deployed* them with the mission and vision of the Great Commission, relying on the power of the Holy Spirit. The result was the unstoppable movement of the kingdom of God, which is still expanding in our world today.

An abundance of leadership instruction is available in contemporary American culture – maybe an overabundance. Some of it contains a lot of truth, some a little, and some none. Where truth exists, however, it is God's truth. We can be sure that it came from Him. I've studied much of the literature on leadership – both secular and Christian – and I am convinced that what is honorable and true in all of it is found first in the Word of God.

How do secular people discover and use God's truth? By what we call 'common grace'. God allows unbelievers to understand and implement that which is true and good even though they may use it for their own purposes rather than for His glory. In my studies of God's Word, of leadership literature and by my personal experience in ministry, I have seen five important habits affirmed. These five habits are absolutely crucial to being a multiplication leader, and to the vision of restoring the church to its God-ordained position as a leadership factory and distribution center.[1]

Leaders are Insatiable Learners

Biblical leaders have a hunger to learn. It's an almost unquenchable drive, and it reflects the scriptural instruction that we are to seek wisdom, which begins with the proper fear of God (Ps. 111:10; Prov. 9:10). From that foundation, we are to grow in our knowledge of the Lord, His Word, His ways, and the world He created.

A God-centered search for wisdom and knowledge honors the Lord, and it's as old as His creation. 'The LORD possessed me [wisdom] at the beginning of His work, the first of His acts of old. Ages ago I [wisdom] was set up, at the first, before the beginning of the earth.' (Prov. 8:22-23) The quest for wisdom and knowledge can be a useful tool for the Lord's work and His glory when it's God-centered. 'Take my instruction instead of silver,' advises Proverbs 8:10, 'and knowledge rather than choice gold.'

---

1. One of the books that stimulated my thinking on this is *The Leadership Engine* by Noel Tichy (New York: Harper Business, 1997).

God doesn't want us to squander our time on knowledge for knowledge's sake. That dishonors Him and makes the pursuit of knowledge idolatry. And it's easy to embrace the idol of knowledge in our information age. Pleasure reading. Surfing the Internet. Watching television, motion pictures, documentaries. All can be useful and at times recreationally restful – if our approach to them is God-centered. But to maximize leadership learning, we need more than mere factual knowledge – we need biblical wisdom, which is the God-given skill of applying knowledge to our lives.

Don't make the mistake of leaning just on what you have already learned, which is evidence of personal arrogance. Such prideful neglect of learning inevitably produces lazy and ineffective leaders. And don't be too busy to keep learning. The old adage is true: 'Don't put the urgent before the important', and here's another one for you: 'While you seek to know all about it, don't be a know-it-all.' Remember, effective leaders are not 'know-it-alls' but effective leaders do have a passion to 'know-it-all'.

Was Jesus a learner? Absolutely: 'Jesus increased in wisdom, and in stature, and in favor with God and man.' (Luke 2:52) Jesus was fully God and therefore omniscient as God the Son, but He was also fully man. And as the Son of Man He intentionally 'increased in wisdom'. So as a biblical leader, you should seek to fulfill your hunger to learn and do so joyfully and with anticipation of how what you are learning will increase your ability to honor the Lord in your ministry. Obviously, study and research – even of Christian works – should not replace your personal time in the Word of God. But you should supplement it with the contributions of the 'pastors and teachers' that have been a much-needed gift from Christ to the church through the ages (Eph. 4:11).

As you organize a plan for ongoing learning, you'll want to take into account your personal learning style. For instance, you may include formal classroom study and small group discussion sessions to your growth plan, or you may find articles, audio programs, or films useful. But remember that most serious research is based upon book-length treatments of subject matter. Here are some suggestions for a diverse categorical foundation for continued learning:

- Commentaries, language tools, and theological journals
- Biographies and histories
- Apologetics and evangelism
- Periodicals
- Devotional commentaries and books
- Communication and/or leadership works
- Contemporary issues, politics, cultural developments
- Regularly scheduled conferences and retreats thoughtfully selected
- An annual sabbatical (one to four weeks) for study, meditation, reflection, writing, prayer, and fasting – formally planned, structured with accountability, and *not* a substitute for a family vacation. (My sabbatical is three weeks in length with identifiable objectives and a report to the elders at its conclusion.)

A large following does not necessarily reflect the presence of biblical leadership. A truer test of an effective Bible-based leader lies not with the size of the followership, but with the quality of leaders he or she produces.

Leaders Seize the Learning Moment

There are occasions in life when we are especially teachable, and often the hardest times teach us the most memorable lessons.

That fact is taught in Scripture and affirmed by personal experience. Adversity, failure, challenges, disappointments, and suffering all hold severe mercies – treasuries of wisdom for those who are humble enough to learn from them. 'Count it all joy, my brothers, when you meet trials of various kinds, for you know that the testing of your faith produces steadfastness. And let steadfastness have its full effect, that you may be perfect and complete, lacking in nothing.' (James 1:2-4) Similar truths are also driven home in Romans 5:3-4: 'More than that, we rejoice in our sufferings, knowing that suffering produces endurance, and endurance produces character, and character produces hope.'

The hardships of life, even when they're self-inflicted, can be transformed by God into growth in righteousness. One of the challenges of learning from those special, difficult teaching moments is that they're also the times when we're most apt to engage in self-preservation and self-pity. We must be careful that our tendency toward self-protection in those hard moments doesn't block us from learning God's appointed lessons.

Seldom do we learn much in times of affluence and prosperity. 'God whispers to us in our pleasures ... but shouts to us in our pains,' wrote C. S. Lewis in *The Problem of Pain*.[2] Adversity yielded to the Lord can open the vaults of wisdom if you choose to enter boldly and not retreat fearfully. Don't miss the blessing by blaming others or by giving in to anger or bitterness. Instead, seize the moment, as painful as it may be, and realize that the Lord has just rung the school bell.

Class is in. There are great lessons to learn. Learn them well.

The wife of Jonathan Edwards, in a letter to her daughter after the untimely death of her husband (who had just become the president of the College of New Jersey, now Princeton University), provides a remarkable testimony of how God's grace enables us to learn even in our deepest moments of grief and adversity:

> My very dear child, What shall I say! A holy and good God has covered us with a dark cloud. O that we may kiss the rod, and lay our hands upon our mouths! The Lord has done it. He has made me adore His goodness, that we had [your father] so long. But my God lives; and he has my heart. O what a legacy my husband, and your father, has left us! We are all given to God; and there I am, and love to be. Your affectionate mother, Sarah Edwards.[3]

Leaders Lead Others to Learn

A biblical leader thrives on giving away what he or she has learned by teaching and coaching others. Leaders should enthusiastically

---

2. C. S. Lewis, *The Problem of Pain* (New York: HarperCollins, 2001), p. 91.

3. Elizabeth Dodds, *Marriage to a Difficult Man: The Uncommon Union of Jonathan and Sarah Edwards* (Philadelphia: Westminster Press, 1971), p. 196.

recruit and assemble their team of leaders, train them, and put them to work – and then stand ready to encourage, instruct, disciple, and correct as needed. Great leaders are not only insatiable learners, they are unstoppable teachers, constantly coaching and taking great joy when they see their disciples walking in the truth.

Being a leader who continually teaches and coaches others can be excruciatingly difficult. It can be discouraging. It can be thankless. It can even be dangerous. And it is often exhausting – but it produces an exhilarating joy even at the moment of exhaustion. The scriptural truth that 'it is more blessed to give than to receive' (Acts 20:35) is continually proven true in God-centered, Bible-based leadership

When it's hard, avoid complaining – but don't fake it. You don't have to wear a grin all the time or be 'professionally' upbeat. Mentoring is often hard; just don't make it unnecessarily so. Embrace the joy of the Lord in the gift of being a leader/coach. Savor it gratefully. And when it's appropriate – which is often – demonstrate the joy of your salvation and the pleasure of serving the risen Christ Jesus by equipping the next generation of leaders. 'A glad heart makes a cheerful face,' and 'the cheerful of heart has a continual feast' (Prov. 15:13, 15). If you grow weary or dreary, step back from the fray and go to the Lord for a period of refreshment, healing, and redirection. Make it your daily goal to practice an attitude of gratitude and to seek the contentment and fulfillment that come from a surrendered and obedient heart. Learn to love leadership, out of love for the Leader who called you.

You have known the joy of being a learner, the discipline of seizing your personal learning moments, and the inexplicable joy of giving it away to others as a mentor and coach. That's a cause for great praise to God! You have not only been gifted but you have been made a gift to others.

Leaders Use Memorable Maxims

'Remember who you are and where you are from.'

I can still hear those words a generation later, just as they were delivered by my high school principal. He was a remarkable leader. He seemed to know the name of every student – almost two thousand of us – and he regularly greeted each one of us that way. He led a well-run, highly effective public high school, and he did it with a character-based honor code. No locks were needed on student lockers; the honor code prevented theft. Teachers could leave the classroom during testing; the honor code prevented cheating. Nobody would have dared to physically attack another student; the honor code prevented violence.

The principal kept the standards high, and one effective tool he used was memorable maxims. I remember several, but the one that he used as a foundation for everything else called on us to conduct ourselves in a manner that upheld a good name and honored our families and our school: 'Remember who you are and where you are from.' At our fortieth reunion the first thing out of our mouths to each other was that simple statement. A truly memorable maxim. As a result, our student body pursued living up to that expectation and nobody wanted to undermine it.

Decades later, I visited the same school, and I was shocked. Not only were locks affixed to every locker, but all the doors were locked and equipped with alarms. Police officers patrolled the halls. Instead of the blessings of a self-regulated honor code, the students were basically imprisoned to protect them from one another. The dramatic change was sobering evidence of how our nation had abandoned a biblical worldview that created an ethical perspective on life, as embodied by the words of our high school principal, which called us to integrity, sobriety, honesty, and simply treating others as you would have them treat you. In a word, that was the foundation of our honor code.

Today's leaders have failed us. Our nation has turned from the Lord, and within a single generation the rotten fruit of that rebellion was glaringly obvious in the halls of a public high school. Knowing what the Bible says about sin, that does not amaze me. But what really saddens me is that we are no longer producing leaders with a Christian world- and life-view who are deployed into the various spheres of our society, including the halls of education.

As I made a heartsick appraisal of my old school, I remember thinking, *Everything rises and falls on leadership.* At home, church, school, work, and everywhere, biblical leaders must teach that character indeed does count. And a priceless tool for driving home the appropriate lessons is a memorable maxim.

Did Jesus do that? Did He teach with memorable maxims? Absolutely. Look at the Gospels, and you'll see thirty-two parables, two allegories, six sermons, and countless meaningful observations used by the Lord to teach His followers and us – all containing memorable maxims. You can do it, too, repeating the ones from Christ and other good teachers, or making up your own. It's simply a matter of taking a profound truth and reducing it to a statement that's easy to remember. Pray about it and do it. If you want to effectively exercise biblical leadership, develop the habit of passing on what you've learned with clear, simple, and memorable maxims that can last – and work – for a lifetime.

> Great leaders are not only insatiable learners, they are unstoppable teachers, constantly coaching and taking great joy when they see their disciples walking in the truth.

Leaders Show Others How to Seize Learning Moments

A biblical leader not only makes good use of his own learning moments, but also helps his disciples learn how to do the same. Leaders embrace, encourage, comfort, instruct – and also insist on the discipline of gaining positive outcomes from negative experiences. As in parenting, the application of discipline for learning is usually the most challenging. But it's also vital.

When I was a boy, my dad would occasionally take me for a walk with him. Sometimes as we walked together, he would playfully swing his leg to the side and give me a light kick on the seat of my pants. It always took me by surprise, and I couldn't figure out how he could swing his leg around while walking, but I also couldn't wait until I was a dad and could do the same thing. What I didn't know was that my dad was actually providing for me a wonderful illustration of leadership development.

As I walked along with him, his arm around my shoulder, security and comfort were assured – but then came 'the kick'.

When people experience moments of adversity, failure, and disappointment, our arm must be around them for verbal and physical comfort and encouragement, but at the right time there needs to be a kick in the pants by inquiring, 'What is God trying to teach you in the "university of adversity"? The school bell has just rung and you are in God's classroom, so don't waste this experience but learn what you can from it.'

That's what the discipline of learning is to those we lead and love. When someone is hurting, confused, frustrated, even angry, a Christian leader's rightful inclination is to provide comfort – especially if the leader is a pastor. The importance of following that biblically-based inclination cannot be overemphasized. But neither can the importance of simultaneously implementing and overseeing the discipline of learning. It, too, is an act of love, and often can be even more productive than a hug, a financial gift, or well-spoken words of encouragement.

Remember Hebrews 12:11: 'For the moment all discipline seems painful rather than pleasant, but later it yields the peaceful fruit of righteousness to those who have been trained by it.' If you love those you lead, you will gently but firmly bless them with the discipline of learning when it's appropriate. And you'll stand ready to help them identify and seize other kinds of learning moments when they come. Remember, adversity is a providentially Divine appointment for learning.

Jesus assisted His disciples in seizing their personal learning moments and the Gospels are replete with examples. A number can be found in the Apostle Peter's relationship with the Lord. Perhaps the most memorable occurred after Christ's resurrection. Peter had denied the Lord three times on the night before the crucifixion, but it was not the end of His spiritual journey. After Jesus rose from the dead, He gently confronted Peter on the banks of the Sea of Galilee. The event is reported in John 21:15-18 and, paraphrasing, it goes like this:

> 'Do you love me more than these?' Jesus asked, likely gesturing toward the other disciples because Peter had boasted that even if they deserted the Lord, he would not.
>
> 'Yes, Lord; you know that I love you,' Peter responded.

'Feed my lambs,' Jesus told him, and then asked the question a second time.

Peter gave the same answer: 'Yes, Lord; you know that I love you.'

Jesus replied, 'Tend my sheep,' and then repeated the question a third time – 'Simon, son of John, do you love me?'

Peter was grieved to be asked three times to profess his love. 'Lord, you know everything,' he said; 'you know that I love you.'

Again Jesus said to him, 'Feed my sheep.'

Clearly, Jesus was challenging Peter to seize a crucial learning moment. He had publicly denied Christ three times, and Jesus here allowed Peter to affirm Him three times. The old had gone, the new had come – and Peter experienced the blessing of forgiveness and a new beginning.

Do you think Peter ever forgot that learning moment? It was a painful, humbling experience for him, but it was a learning moment that left him better equipped as a Christian leader. No wonder that when Peter challenges the leaders of the church in 1 Peter 5:1-11, he reminds them that 'God opposes the proud but gives grace to the humble. Humble yourselves, therefore, under the mighty hand of God so that at the proper time He may exalt you.' (1 Pet. 5:5-6)

The next time Peter is recorded as speaking publicly is when he stands before thousands as he preaches the Gospel at Pentecost, and more than three thousand people come to Jesus Christ as Lord and Savior. The Lord breaks those whom he is going to use so that it is His strength in which we boast and not our own. And that is especially true of leaders.

What is God trying to teach you in the 'university of adversity'? The school bell has just rung and you are in God's classroom, so don't waste this experience but learn what you can from it.

Christ the Masterful Multiplication and Mobilization Leader

So, who is the most effective multiplication and mobilization leader that ever lived? Who was incomparable in *defining, developing, and deploying* leaders? Who embodied these five multiplication and mobilization habits better than anyone else? The answer, of course, is Jesus. And if these five habits are not found in Christ's three year ministry strategy of leadership multiplication and mobilization then they should be deemed worthless. But, the fact is, He perfectly embodied all five habits.

- He was an insatiable learner – 'growing in wisdom, stature, favor with God and favor with man' (Luke 2:52).

- He seized His personal learning moments of adversity as He 'learned obedience through what he suffered' (Heb. 5:8).

- He was a relentless coach and mentor.

- He put what He taught in memorable maxims.

- He enabled his disciples to seize their learning moments as evidenced in each of their lives, most notably Peter's – from a charcoal fire in the Garden of Caiaphas where he denied the Lord three times, to another charcoal fire by the Sea of Galilee after the resurrection where he confessed the Lord three times.

'If It Ain't Horse, Carve It Out'

When faithfully practiced, those five habits of biblical leadership can dramatically shape a leader's life and position him or her to be a multiplication leader, which will help enable the Lord's church to once again become a leadership factory and distribution center.

Scripture commands leaders as well as followers to constantly be seeking to grow in the Lord, to live and to lead for Him. 'I have been crucified with Christ,' Paul writes in Galatians 2:20. 'It is no longer I who live, but Christ who lives in me. And the life I now live in the flesh I live by faith in the Son of God, who loved me and gave Himself for me.' Make it your goal to be more like Christ, and you will become a better multiplication leader.

I once heard a story about a New York City reporter who traveled to Virginia's Blue Ridge Mountains to interview an acclaimed wood-carver. The old mountaineer made exquisite horse sculptures, and his craftsmanship had somehow been discovered by the national media.

The reporter was amazed when he examined the extraordinary horses the man had carved from solid blocks of oak. The creations were stunningly beautiful. Their hooves appeared as if suspended in midair, and their manes looked as if they were flowing in the wind.

'How do you do it?' the reporter said to the old man. 'How do you carve such magnificent, lifelike creations from solid blocks of oak?'

'I don't know, son,' the mountaineer replied. 'I just do it.'

Determined to learn the old man's technique, the reporter pried more. 'What's the full story? What is your secret?'

'Sonny, it's no secret,' the craftsman finally explained. 'I just get my knife and a nice block of wood, and I carve out everything that ain't horse.'

Lord, please carve away everything in our lives that ain't Jesus!

Questions for Thought and Discussion

1) How are you currently learning about the Word of God, and specifically about biblical leadership, on a regular basis? How can you improve the quantity and quality of your learning?

2) What are some examples of when you (or someone you know) learned important lessons through times of adversity and difficulty?

3) Search online for 'leadership maxims' and consider some of them. Are they biblical? If so, how could they be helpful to you?

4) 'Faithful are the wounds of a friend,' Proverbs 27:6 says. When others are in need of correction, what are some ways that you can approach them as a friend rather than an enemy?

5) Review some reasons why Jesus was the best multiplication leader of all time, and pray about how you can be more like Him.

3D Leadership
Part 3

The Third Dimension –
Deploying Leaders

Chapter 9

Past, Present, Future

IN Part 1 of this book we learned about how leadership is *defined* biblically, and in Part 2 how leaders can be *developed* in the church. Now we are ready to focus on how they should be *deployed*, and what they actually should be doing as they seek to change the world for God's glory. We talked about the church returning to its role as a leadership factory, but we also want to see it become a distribution center that benefits not just the church, but all of society as well. When products made in a factory are distributed, they are only truly beneficial if they do what they are intended to do. In the remaining chapters we will focus on the work to which Christian leaders are called.

And we start here: effective leaders will *learn from the past, live in the present*, and *look to the future*.

Learning from the Past

When you read the Old Testament, you can't help but notice how many times the work of God for His people was memorialized: sometimes by piling up stones, sometimes with a psalm or song, and sometimes with a meal, like the Passover. Why did they do this? God wanted them to bring their children back to those historic moments and teach them what great things their God had done, so they could learn from the past to strengthen them in the present and impact the future. Since 'Jesus Christ is the same yesterday and today and forever' (Heb. 13:8), one of the best ways to see His glory is by looking at what He has done 'yesterday'. As we are 'beholding the glory of the Lord' in the past, we will be 'transformed into the same image from one degree of glory to another' (2 Cor. 3:18).

God's people today have been blessed with many classic examples of Godly men and women in history. As is often said in Christian circles, history is really *His*-story. We don't want to be preoccupied with the past or live in the past, but there is much to be learned from it.

Consider George Washington. He was no deist, contrary to modern humanist propaganda, but a devout believer whose faith sustained him in the darkest days of the American Revolution.[1] At one point in the war – the winter of 1777–1778 – the future surely appeared grim to Washington and to the Continental Army he commanded. The British had driven them from New York, across New Jersey, and into Pennsylvania. The nation's fledgling capital, Philadelphia, had been captured. The Pennsylvania State House, where the Declaration of Independence had been signed, was occupied by British troops. The Continental Congress had been forced to flee the city. Washington's army was ragged, hungry, unpaid, and left shivering in their winter camp at Valley Forge, Pennsylvania.

Many believed that American victory was impossible, including some of the nation's leading clergymen. Most notably, George Washington's Pastor in Philadelphia, who had prayed the opening prayer of the Continental Congress. It had implored him to surrender in the gruesome winter of the American Revolution. Yet, Washington was a man of faith, and he would not give up. He was determined to persevere despite the mighty hosts arrayed against him. And he did. He used the bitter months in winter camp to drill his soldiers, inspiring them and encouraging them to believe that they could indeed prevail. Out of his own pocket he paid chaplains to conduct worship services. When the army emerged from Valley Forge in the spring, it was better than ever and prepared to face the worst that the enemy had to offer.

---

1. For an insightful and documented analysis of the impact of Christianity in the life of George Washington, I recommend the epic study *George Washington's Sacred Fire* by Dr Peter Lillback (Providence Forum Press, 2006).

Eventually, many of the same soldiers who had limped through the snow at Valley Forge were present to experience what had once seemed unthinkable: the surrender of Lord Cornwallis' British army at Yorktown. Long before that final victory, when defeat was looming, George Washington firmly clung to a belief in the providence of God. 'The Hand of providence has been so conspicuous in all this,' he wrote in 1778, 'that he must be worse than an infidel that lacks faith, and more than wicked, that has not gratitude enough to acknowledge his obligations.'[2]

What lessons can we learn from Washington's example? Christian leaders must equip themselves with the armor of God, take up the weapons of God, and stand firm. We cannot expect followers to go beyond their leaders. Because Christ has defeated Satan and the kingdom of darkness at the cross, we may confidently lead our people forward. And when they are discouraged, by God's grace they will see that their leaders are confident in the Lord because they have learned their lessons well. The battle is not ours but His, and He who has won the victory will do it again in us and through us.

As you seek to continually learn from the past, in order to lead in the present and into the future, I suggest the models you study and emulate should primarily come from among those who have lived and died in years past. Why do I say this? Because the last chapters in the stories of people like that have already been written, and we know how they ended up. When you pick models from the past, there is no doubt that they finished well – the verdict is already in on whether they will persevere to the end. With those who are still living, however, no matter how admirable they may seem, there is still a chance they might end up being 'disqualified' at some point, to use Paul's terminology in 1 Corinthians 9:27. In that verse the Apostle says: 'I discipline my body and keep it under control, lest after preaching to others I myself should be disqualified.'

In the 1970s, a pastor in San Francisco was so admired for his multi-ethnic ministry and service to the poor that California

---

2. William J. Johnson, *George Washington the Christian* (New York: Abingdon Press, 1919), pp. 119-20.

governor Ronald Reagan wrote him a commendation letter, and First Lady Rosalyn Carter visited his church and spoke from the pulpit. Reagan later regretted his commendation, and Carter her visit, because that pastor was Jim Jones, the cultist who would kill over 900 of his followers with poisoned Kool-Aid in Guyana, South America in 1978. In a similar way, someone living today might unfortunately end up being the opposite of what you should admire. But if you get your models from the Bible and from history, you don't have to worry about that happening. You can know that they finished strong.

> When you pick models from the past, there is no doubt that they finished well – the verdict is already in on whether they will persevere to the end.

Living in the Present

Effective leaders learn from the past, but they refuse to live in the past. Nor are they paralyzed in life waiting for the future. Instead, their primary focus is on fulfilling their mission and calling in the present.

In 1 Chronicles 12:32, leaders from Issachar are commended for being 'men who had understanding of the times, to know what Israel ought to do.' And Acts 13:36 says this about another great Old Testament leader: 'David, after he had served the purpose of God in his own generation, fell asleep and was laid with his fathers.' The two key phrases in that verse are 'served the purpose of God' and 'in his own generation'. David had a call and mission from God, and at his best he was a leader who fulfilled God's purposes and benefited his people by providing exactly what they needed at the time. David himself surely knew the history of his people – past lessons of how God had worked over time – and he certainly cared about the future, but his primary focus was to fulfill 'God's purpose in his own generation'.

Like Esther, who was raised up 'for such a time as this' (Esther 4:14), God has a time and a place for all His leaders. So to be effective, they must know the Word of God *and* the world around them – living in the present for God's glory. Knowing the Word of God equips us to penetrate the culture with the transforming power of truth while anticipating the impact of God's unstoppable Gospel of grace. It will change people and the world in which they live. But if we wade into the waves of the world without knowing the Word, we can expect a pounding – something I learned as a youthful believer.

I became a Christian during my time in college, and as a 'new creation' in Christ (2 Cor. 5:17), I developed a vigor to learn that I never had before. I also attempted to proclaim Christ boldly – and sometimes rashly. I was one of about 300 students enrolled in a psychology class taught by a graduate student who routinely attacked the Bible and the Lord. So I spoke up. The discussions that resulted from my attempt to defend the faith displayed my passion for the Lord, but also revealed my obvious need for more discipleship and time in the Word. The Lord sometimes blessed my attempts to make a good defense despite my shortcomings, but I also often took a beating. I remember standing outside the psychology building after class one day, fielding questions from dozens of fellow students concerning the exchange they had witnessed between the teacher and me. My heart was right, but I needed the maturity and wisdom that comes from investing time in the Word and being discipled by a mature believer. Did God produce fruit through me, and often in spite of me? Certainly. He was faithful, but I could have represented Him better in those days if I had been more well-grounded in His Word.

Just as we must study the Word, we must also study the world. Doing so enables a leader to understand the 'spirit of the age' – the values and perspectives of the day. That is necessary to become a change agent for the Lord. Remember that a Christian leader is to shape the culture; the culture must not be allowed to shape the leader. Therefore, we must be alert, constantly examining ourselves lest we become like the world as we are attempting to impact the world. And it is easy to accommodate the world, even when we have the best of motives.

An example is how we can lose our focus in corporate worship. Contemporary American culture has two obsessions: entertainment and freedom of choice. In an attempt to evangelize (a good motive), many churches have trumped worship with those obsessions in the name of evangelism, thus creating the oxymoron of 'seeker-centered worship'. But instead of that imbalance, we should be worshiping in a God-centered way that draws seekers to Christ.

We can also be imbalanced the other way. Some churches today are so disinterested in evangelism (turning the Great Commission into the 'Great Omission') that they have become distant islands toward which seekers must swim alone in order to be rescued. Even if seekers make it to that distant shore, they find themselves in a religious museum dedicated to bygone achievements rather than a movement of God's saving and transforming grace. That is why many churches have swung the pendulum too far the other way, and in the name of attracting seekers, are using methods of evangelism that actually become counterproductive to the message of the Gospel. Both extremes illustrate the fact that even the best of motives, if attached to unbiblical practices, can produce less than desirable results.

Remember, biblical worship is God-centered, not seeker-centered *or* believer-centered. Like the culture around them, many of today's seekers and believers are focused on being entertained. On the other hand, many religious people insist on stifling joy in the name of reverence. Genuine biblically-defined, God-centered worship will not accommodate either of those extremes, but will attract seekers and encourage believers. Authentic God-centered worship, according to 1 Corinthians 14:25, can cause an unbeliever to fall on his face 'and declare that God is really among you'.

God is 'really among you' when *He* is the center of worship – not believers, and not even seekers. 'Not to us, O LORD, not to us,' says Psalm 115:1, 'but to Your name give glory for the sake of Your steadfast love and Your faithfulness!' Lovingly pursuing the lost that they might become seekers of Christ is not accomplished by pandering to the world or abandoning Gospel truths. Today's sermon titles, book topics, and music lyrics often resemble the titles of popular magazines: *Self, Us, We, Me*, and *People*. In the name of evangelism, much of the contemporary American church attempts to make Christianity simply one more self-esteem-boosting therapeutic model with Jesus as a genie in the bottle who offers health, wealth, power, and purpose.

God does not exist to give us possessions, or even purpose. He *is* our purpose and we are His possession. Even more, He is our passion, and His Gospel calls us to the glory of dying to self and living for Christ. We must understand the prevailing culture in order to address it, but we must avoid being like the world even as we are in it. Christian leaders must be like the ones in the tribe of Issachar who had an 'understanding of the times, to know what Israel ought to do' (1 Chron. 12:32).

> Remember that a Christian leader is to shape the culture; the culture must not be allowed to shape the leader.

Leading to the Future

Grounded in the Word, aware of the surrounding culture, and tutored from history, effective leaders seek to impact the future. Worldly leaders can perceive the trajectory of the culture and take advantage of it for their own benefit, but we need men and women who are able to change the trajectory of the culture for the glory of the Lord and the good of others. Let's consider some ways that can happen.

Impart a biblical vision

Effective leaders must avoid 'the paralysis of analysis'. It is certainly true that you should not begin before you know where you are going and what you want to accomplish. But some leaders become incapacitated by indecision. They fail to advance because they fear that they don't have enough information to make a decision, and therefore they are constantly vacillating. Effective, biblically-based leaders are not indecisive; they have a vision that is biblically defined and culturally connected. With the power of the Gospel and the pre-eminence of Christ in deed and word, they seek to act on it without undue hesitation.

A future-oriented leader has a vision that grows out of knowing the Word of God, studying the past, and understanding his or her present location and generation. Equipped with the indwelling presence and power of the Spirit of God, a leader is then positioned to impart that vision to others. Where is God leading the church? The leader's family? The leader's ministry or business? You cannot begin a journey, much less take others with you, unless you know where you are going.

When I step up on the first tee to play a round of golf, I have two swing thoughts (actually two prayer requests): 'Lord, please do not let me embarrass myself in front of everyone,' and 'Lord, please allow me to find this ball after I hit it.' When Tiger Woods steps on the first tee, I'm sure those are not his swing thoughts. In his mind, he is already on the green, putting for a birdie. To be there on the green, there is a certain place in the fairway where he needs to land his tee shot. Now he is ready to hit his drive off the tee. Lesson? *In leadership you begin from the end.*

'Lord, why am I here in this leadership position? To what destination are you taking us?' That is the vision, and it must be continually and passionately imparted to those whom you are leading.

Be a self-starter who values humility

By God's grace and the power of the Holy Spirit, effective leaders are self-starters. Because they are nourished by the love of God in Christ and guided by the truth of His Word, they have an innate desire to do their best at all times. The result is they are constantly seeking genuine spiritual growth in life and ministry to honor the Lord. They 'work out [their] own salvation with fear and trembling,' as Philippians 2:12 says, and they have a strong *ambition* to be pleasing to the Lord in their ministries (see 2 Cor. 5:9 NASB).

But the hard work and ambition of a truly effective Christian leader is always tempered with the humility of a servant's heart. That is why biblical leaders are not threatened when their ministry or organization establishes performance evaluations, but instead welcome the opportunity for accountability and improvement. They are aware of God's numerous Scriptural admonitions that 'He tears down the prideful and exalts the humble.' Some leaders exalt themselves and then pray for humility, but the Scripture tells us to do the opposite: 'Humble yourselves before the Lord, and He will exalt you.' (James 4:10)

One of my most treasured mentors is a very powerful preacher who recounts this 'encouragement' to humility: One Sunday, as he drove home from church with his wife, he thought about the sermon he had preached that day. It was perhaps the best sermon he had ever delivered, he told himself. Turning to his wife, a loving and supportive spouse – and an honest, perceptive woman – he posed a question that begged for a U-turn back to a state of humility. Cheerfully, his wife assisted him.

'Honey,' he asked her, 'how many great preachers do you think there are in the United States? I mean, how many *really* great preachers?' His wife looked at him for a moment, then blandly replied: 'Honey, I don't know how many there are. But I do know this: there is one less than you think.'

Establish personal accountability and evaluation

In Chapter 3 I discussed the need for personal accountability in order to meet the qualifications for entering church leadership, and it is also important if you are going to *continue* in that role. All leaders who are effective in the long term have found a way to make sure that they are accountable to others. Perhaps it is an accountability partner, a group or the church elders. They meet regularly for prayer, sharing, caring, and self-improvement before the Lord.

It is also wise for a leader to have a formal evaluation team composed of insightful elders or other church leaders. The team should meet regularly to evaluate and offer encouragement, observation, and instruction. It's good for the leader, it's good for the group, and it will be good for the church or organization.

> Worldly leaders can perceive the trajectory of the culture and take advantage of it for their own benefit, but we need men and women who are able to change the trajectory of the culture for the glory of the Lord and the good of others.

Following is a list of diagnostic maxims that can be asked and discussed regularly in this more formal process of evaluation.[3]

---

3. These are adapted from my book *From Embers to a Flame: How God Can Revitalize Your Church* (Phillipsburg, NJ: P & R Publishing, 2008), pp. 173-5.

Leaders can rate themselves (perhaps from one to five points) on how well each statement applies to them, and then the evaluators can discuss their observations with them.

I take risks, but don't deny reality.

I am innovative, but not ridiculous or novel just to gain attention.

I take charge, but do not oppress people.

I have high expectations that stretch others and raise the bar for all, but don't set people up for failure by demanding the impossible.

I maintain a positive attitude, but stay in touch with reality.

I create opportunities for success in small things that encourage others to tackle the greater challenges.

I lead from the front, but stay in touch with those who are following and supporting.

I give public credit for success to my people, but take responsibility myself for any failure or setback.

I plan my work and work my plan, and always remember that my plan and my work are people.

I establish priorities in my leadership plans, and stay with them.

I establish accountability for myself and for my subordinates.

I raise the bar of performance on myself.

I avoid bitterness and animosity towards those who are in opposition.

I avoid the luxury of rationalizations and public blaming of subordinates.

I clearly communicate my objectives and methods, as well as my expectations for others.

I ensure agreement and support by subordinates on vision, goals, philosophy, and tactics.

I am aware of my subordinates' preferences, strengths and weaknesses.

I develop thoughtful loyalty from leader to follower, as well as from follower to leader.

I am courageous, yet avoid being foolhardy in the name of bravery.

I develop clear objectives and overall strategy, but at the same time maintain the ability to be flexible.

Focus on the fundamentals

In his autobiography, *My Story*, the great professional golfer Jack Nicklaus revealed something very interesting about his game. Every year throughout his spectacular career, Nicklaus went back home to Ohio to spend time with a local golf pro named Jack Grout, who was Nicklaus's longtime mentor and golf teacher. Together they would go to the practice tee, where Nicklaus always began the new season with the same request: 'Jack, teach me how to play golf.' Grout would respond by going through the basics of the game as if the great Nicklaus was an untrained amateur. They would play the course that way, with Nicklaus again in the role of the student, learning the fundamentals of the game from his teacher.

Jack Nicklaus knew that the key to playing great golf lay in focusing on the fundamentals. Christian leadership is the same: greatness and effectiveness come from continually refining and building upon the basics with a commitment to excellence.

Another similar example is Derek Jeter, one of the best shortstops to ever play baseball. Jeter would go to spring training every year and take hundreds of ground balls and swings in the batting cage daily, preparing for the upcoming season. He did that even after winning his five World Series titles, not just when he had been hurt or had had a bad season.

Greatness seldom is a matter of exotic ingenuity, but usually flows from the ability of a leader to stay focused on the fundamentals and execute them with excellence.

Discipline yourself for the purpose of Godliness

In my study of great leaders an incontrovertible fact has surfaced – every great leader has uncommon standards and habits of discipline for themselves in the priorities they have established in their lives.

Discipline doesn't come easy to us saved sinners, especially in a sinful world. For most of us, it is a lifelong struggle. But it's a battle worth fighting. Why? Because discipline is a key factor in life and leadership, and especially when our goal is to lead far into the future. Continuing to grow in the Lord through His Word requires established habits of self-discipline including a regular private prayer life and family life of prayer and worship embedded in the church life of prayer and worship which impacts your work and ministry habits. And gratefully it will also transform everything else worthwhile and important in our lives. Leaders who follow the biblical model of leadership always become self-disciplined and intentionally seek to remain so.

Remember, however, that a disciplined life is not an attempt to earn God's love. Our God has given that love freely in Christ – 'We love because he first loved us.' (1 John 4:19) A disciplined life is one way that we show our love to God, and one way that we worship Him, by seeking to be consistently faithful in fulfilling His call on our lives.

Great leaders – God-centered leaders – refuse to squander their lives to the whims of culture, the fads of the day, the ways of the world. They learn from the past without living in the past. They live in the present without accommodating it, and they lead to the future without waiting for it. To do so, they learn God's Word, understand the surrounding culture, and seek to impart a biblical mission and vision as grace-filled self-starters – who seek to be accountable, focus on the basics, and live a disciplined lifestyle.

In short, truly great leaders seek to live according to the familiar advice of Proverbs 3:5: 'Trust in the LORD with all your heart, and do not lean on your own understanding. In all your ways acknowledge Him, and he will make straight your paths.' That is not simply a pleasant homily. It is a proverbial promise of wisdom from the God of the ages.

Believe His Word and get ready for some amazing experiences as you fulfill the tasks of Christian leadership that God has outlined in His Word. In the next chapter, we will find out more about three of the most important roles He has planned for you to play in the church and in society.

Questions for Thought and Discussion

1) Consider further the business analogy of a 'factory' and 'distribution center' mentioned at the beginning of the chapter, and how it relates to leadership in the church. For example, how are the two dependent upon each other, and how can the church 'distribute' good leaders into other churches and spheres of society?

2) What are some examples of good and bad leadership from the past that we can learn from?

3) What are some ways in which you can be educated about the culture around you without being unduly influenced by it?

4) What does 'future grace' mean, and why is it important and helpful? (If you do an internet search on the term, you'll see that Dr John Piper has some good online information on the topic, and also a book about it that you could read if you want to learn more.)

5) What are some dangers of neglecting the past and the future as you live and minister in the present? What about over-emphasizing them? Take some time to pray that you will have a balance between the past, present and future in your life and ministry.

Chapter 10

Shepherds, Servants, Superintendents

A FACTORY can put out an abundance of polished products, but if there is no need for them in the society, all that work will be pointless. Likewise, the leaders a church produces must be deployed to serve a necessary purpose and provide an important and biblical contribution in their culture.

One big problem in our day, as Jesus observed about His own, is that multitudes are 'harassed and helpless, like sheep without a shepherd' (Matt. 9:36). Another is that most leadership in our world is more concerned with what they can gain for themselves than what they can give to others. And the leaders we do have, even those with the best of motives, are often glaringly incompetent in their administrative skills.

So we need to raise up and send out qualified leaders who will do the work of shepherds, servants, and superintendents. Then the church will not only be a leadership factory for our age, but also a successful distribution center, meeting the greatest needs of the people around us as defined by the Word of God and as addressed by Christian leadership through deployed Christian leaders.

A Christian Leader is a Shepherd

Are you a rancher or a shepherd?

What is the difference, you might ask, and why does it matter? Good questions. It matters a lot if you're a Christian leader. Christian leaders are shepherds who lead from the front not ranchers who drive from the rear. Ranchers drive herds from the

151

rear and with the whip; shepherds lead flocks from the front with their voices. It's that simple. Ranchers crack the whip and create fear. Shepherds call the sheep by name and set the pace for them.

I once saw this firsthand in Israel. In the countryside outside Jerusalem, I noticed a flock of sheep in the distance. As I watched their Bedouin shepherd, I realized that he was not driving the flock from behind, but was leading it from the front. His rod and staff were not used for beating the sheep, but were available for tending and defending them. I could hear him singing and occasionally calling those who were wandering away. The sheep knew his voice, and he knew his sheep – he called them by name – and they calmly followed him.

It's no accident that the Lord refers to His beloved people as sheep and not cattle, nor is it accidental that He delights in picturing His leadership as a Good Shepherd. Go to the high country of Wyoming today and you'll sometimes see a white dot on a faraway mountain meadow. It's a sheep wagon – the shepherd's home. The shepherd will stay with his flock in the remote upland meadows for the entire summer, isolated by choice from the rest of the world, simply to take care of his sheep.

The ultimate model

Being a good shepherd requires a sacrificial lifestyle. The Lord taught us that, and much more, when He discussed the analogy in John 10:1-11:

> 'Truly, truly, I say to you, he who does not enter the sheepfold by the door but climbs in by another way, that man is a thief and a robber. But he who enters by the door is the shepherd of the sheep. To him the gatekeeper opens. The sheep hear his voice, and he calls his own sheep by name and leads them out. When he has brought out all his own, he goes before them, and the sheep follow him, for they know his voice. A stranger they will not follow, but they will flee from him, for they do not know the voice of strangers.' This figure of speech Jesus used with them, but they did not understand what he was saying to them.
>
> So Jesus again said to them, 'Truly, truly, I say to you, I am the door of the sheep. All who came before me are thieves and robbers, but the sheep did not listen to them. I am the door. If anyone enters

by me, he will be saved and will go in and out and find pasture. The thief comes only to steal and kill and destroy. I came that they may have life and have it abundantly. I am the good shepherd. The good shepherd lays down his life for the sheep'. (John 10:6-11)

What an extraordinary model. Let's look at it more carefully.

First, a shepherd knows his sheep, and they 'know his voice'. Obviously, the Lord does this to perfection in ways far beyond what we are able to do as sinful, finite leaders. Think, however, about how Christian leaders can apply this model in leading their flocks. Knowing your sheep so well that they know your voice requires an investment of *love*, *time*, and *attention*: a love for the Lord and your people that motivates you to exercise your call; the time necessary to know the needs of your people and to be there for them; and the attention necessary to respond to their needs promptly and consistently.

Do you have so many sheep in your flock that it's impossible for you to do that personally? Then it's your responsibility to reproduce and develop new leaders who extend Christ's shepherding to His people, so that everyone may be cared for by a competent shepherd/leader. This is why in the Bible every time you see the word 'elder' (the ordained office of shepherd) and the word 'church' (the flock of God), elder will be plural and church will be singular. To multiply effective shepherd leaders in the church, you will have to lead your fellow leaders in learning the heart and life of a shepherd and how to multiply and mobilize more shepherds.

Also, while a false shepherd will abandon his sheep in hard times, a true shepherd will lay down his life for his sheep at all times. Again, Christ is our model, and Christ-centered leadership stands in sharp contrast to self-centered leadership. The world's models are self-centered and manipulative, which leads to using and abusing followers. Worldly leadership is all about power, control, and personal promotion. It's a cattle drive. Sometimes it's effective in reaching a goal, but inevitably it's all about the leader, and those who pay the cost are the followers. Whether it succeeds or fails, it usually leaves behind human wreckage. The biblical model of leadership must be distinctively different. It's Christ-centered, not self-centered. The Christian leader who practices

Christ-centered leadership shepherds his sheep by positioning himself in front of his flock to lead and set the pace for it.

The dramatic contrast between the false shepherd and the good shepherd is that the good shepherd pays the cost for the sheep while the false shepherd seeks to profit from the sheep, and therefore the sheep pay the price for the shepherd's comfort.

> A leader is responsible to reproduce and develop new leaders who extend Christ's shepherding to His people, so that everyone may be cared for by a competent shepherd/leader.

Good and bad examples

I saw both kinds of leadership clearly displayed in the midst of a terrible tragedy. On August 24, 1992, Hurricane Andrew slammed into southern Florida. It was a Category 5 storm, and it hit with the power of an atomic blast. It killed forty people, left a quarter-million people homeless, damaged or destroyed more than eighty thousand businesses, and caused more than $30 billion in damages.

I was with a team of believers who traveled to the area to help in the wake of the storm. Homestead, Florida City, and South Miami looked like war zones. We connected with a number of churches in the area. At one of the churches the congregational leadership had established a command center, and the pastor was in charge of directing the response. The church secured status reports on families in the neighborhood – non-members as well as members – and a team of leaders prioritized the needs. Another team gathered and organized available resources. A smaller team matched the resources with the needs, and then other teams were dispatched to help, providing prayer, food, water, shelter, and other necessities, along with personal encouragement. They did great work at a great cost to themselves.

The pastor who directed the operation, as well as the other leaders involved, had all suffered personal losses of some kind, yet they put aside their own needs for those whom they served. They did great work for the Lord, their congregation, and their community. It was a powerful witness – shepherding at its best. God's people were cared for, the community was ministered to, and the world saw the witness when a special was aired on ABC television about the church and the ministry. And it all began with sacrificial shepherding.

Unfortunately, another pastor's response was a dramatic contrast. We showed up at his church to help, but no one was there. So we made our way to the pastor's home, and no one was there either. Some from the area had been evacuated before the hurricane, but many residents who were not able to leave and those residents who were now returning – including his members – were there but he was not. He chose to remain elsewhere. Certainly it was important for him to make sure that his family was in a place of safety and was receiving care. But what about his flock? He failed to be there when they needed him the most, and when he could have provided leadership to help and inspire his surrounding neighborhood. It was the opposite of sacrificial, Christ-centered shepherding. His flock, leaderless, was left to depend solely on themselves and others. You can be assured that if Christ Himself had been the Shepherd of that flock He would have been there no matter what the cost to Himself. That is the kind of shepherd leaders that are needed in the church and from the church into the world.

Thankfully the good providence of God led our team there, and we were able to help. But that pastor missed an opportunity to manifest the Chief Shepherd's love for his people and establish a caring relationship with them, which he could have built upon in the future. The shepherd had taken care of himself and avoided much of the pain that his flock had experienced, but by doing so he also forfeited the chance to be Christ's instrument at a key time in their lives.

The most famous psalm

Think about the familiar, comforting words of Psalm 23, and notice the model established for Christian leaders there:

> The LORD is my shepherd; I shall not want.
>   He makes me lie down in green pastures.
> He leads me beside still waters.
>   He restores my soul.

He leads me in paths of righteousness
    for his name's sake.
Even though I walk through the valley of the
        shadow of death,
    I will fear no evil,
for you are with me;
        your rod and your staff,
        they comfort me.
You prepare a table before me
    in the presence of my enemies;
you anoint my head with oil;
    my cup overflows.
Surely goodness and mercy shall follow me
    all the days of my life,
and I shall dwell in the house of the LORD forever.

Remember that a shepherd's rod and staff are not for beating or prodding the sheep, but for protecting and rescuing them. The blunt end of the staff is used to drive away predators, and the hook on the other end – the crook of the rod – is used to pull them from danger. The Good Shepherd at the risk of everything will use the rod and staff to comfort the sheep by 'tending and defending'. That's why the passage says the rod and staff are a comfort. The passage also illustrates the shepherd's commitment to feed the sheep and nourish them in 'green pastures' and to rest them beside 'still waters'.

When tending to the needs of the sheep, the Good Shepherd focuses on the priority work of restoring the soul. The sheep have been rescued from potential harm and are assured of everlasting victory through Christ. That's why the familiar 'valley' verse describes death as a 'shadow', something that is temporary and passing for the believer. Death is only a shadow of what it was before it was overcome by one who laid down his life for the sheep.

In following this model, shepherd leaders will intentionally commit to addressing the needs of their people ('Surely goodness and mercy shall follow me all the days of my life') and particularly their spiritual needs ('I shall dwell in the house of the LORD forever').

A Christian Leader is a Servant

The idea of servant leadership is a familiar one that, sadly, is often taught but seldom practiced. Many Christians smile and claim to be servants – until they're actually treated like one.

A ministry leader in Latin America authored a book on servant leadership that sold more than a million copies in the Third World. While it was embraced there, it received very little interest in the United States. A publisher asked the author why he thought this fundamental truth of leadership was so popular in other places but not in America. The author replied sadly that American ministry leaders want to rule rather than serve – they'd rather be 'lords of all' than 'servants of all'.

If that's true, then we're surely leading by the values of the world instead of the principles of the Word, because Scripture is clear about this matter. Consider, for example, the kind of leadership shown to us in John 13. On the night described there, Jesus administered the last old-covenant meal of renewal – the Passover. Then as the living, eternal Passover Lamb, He instituted the new-covenant meal of renewal – the Lord's Supper. Jesus Christ, God in human form, was about to take the punishment that we deserve for our sins as the unblemished Lamb of the Passover. And by His atoning sacrifice all who believe in Him would be saved. He also left us with an unmistakable model of Christian servant leadership when 'He laid aside his outer garments, and taking a towel, tied it around his waist. Then He poured water into a basin and began to wash the disciples' feet and to wipe them with the towel that was wrapped around Him.' (John 13:4-5)

There it is for all of us to see and emulate. Jesus Christ, the Lord God of the ages, did what a household servant was supposed to have done. He took a basin of water and washed the filthy feet of a dozen sandal-wearing men. It was not too lowly for Him, and it was not by accident. He did it to teach an unforgettable lesson to His disciples, and to us. Christian leadership is not lording it over anyone; it's being willing to serve everyone.

The idea of servant leadership is a familiar one that, sadly, is often taught but seldom practiced. Many Christians smile and claim to be servants – until they're actually treated like one.

Servant leadership does not require much instruction (beyond the exhortation to be servants), but it does require motivation and humility. Instead of striving to be served, Christian leaders strive to serve. And what a dramatic impression servant leadership can make in our self-serving culture, even in little ways.

I once played a round of golf with the prominent CEO of a major multinational bank. I had been told that he was a committed believer, and I soon became a beneficiary of and witness to his faithful Christ-centered and Christ-like servant leadership. He was a pleasant, friendly fellow, but it wasn't his edifying words that impressed me – it was his seemingly small gestures. On every hole, this influential, wealthy, and acclaimed executive not only repaired his ball mark on the green according to golf etiquette, but also repaired everyone else's before we arrived. Not only that, he routinely marked and cleaned everyone's golf ball before he gave it back to them. These were small acts that revealed a large servant's heart. So it was no surprise when I later found out that in his business this Christian leader pioneered many creative programs to benefit his employees and customers, including one that enabled the working poor to purchase a home at a reasonable price with an appropriate loan structure.

If you are willing to take the posture of a slave (Greek *doulos*, also translated 'servant') toward God and others, you too can be deployed to make a significant impact on the world around you.

A Christian Leader is a Superintendent

Some leaders have the commitment to be a shepherd and the heart of a servant, but they're ineffective because they fail to bless those under their care by providing superintendent leadership. They just aren't willing to do the planning and administration necessary for life-changing leadership effectiveness. But that's also a part of God's call to leaders: to be overseers who superintend people, policies, and processes for the advancement of God's kingdom.

Scripture makes it clear in 1 Timothy 3:4-5 that a good leader is a superintendent, beginning with excellence in family management, which positions him for effective church management: 'He must manage his own household well, with all dignity keeping his children submissive, for if someone does not know how to manage his own household, how will he care for God's church?'

How do you as a leader know how to be a superintendent in your home? It starts with learning what God expects you to provide for others as revealed in His Word. If you're a husband, for instance, you're commanded to love your wife 'as Christ loved the church' (Eph. 5:25). This means that you reflect Christ as Prophet, Priest, and King. As 'prophet' of the home, you're expected to promote the spiritual development of your family and conduct yourself in a Christ-like manner in thought, word, and deed. As 'priest', you're to provide for your family's needs even at the expense of your own with the selfless heart of a servant. As 'king', you have the responsibility to lovingly and respectfully guide your wife and children.

What about in the church? The same is true: leaders must know from God's Word what He expects them to provide as they superintend the flock of God. A key part of this is the provision of what are commonly called the 'means of grace', a term which refers to the regular practices through which people come to Christ and grow in Christ. They are worth taking some extra time to consider, because good superintendents, both in the home and the church, make sure that everyone under their leadership is able to benefit from these 'means of grace'. So what are they?

The Word of God. According to Romans 10:17: 'faith comes from hearing, and hearing through the word of Christ.' The priority of exposing God's people to God's Word is a recurring theme throughout Scripture. 'For since, in the wisdom of God, the world did not know God through wisdom, it pleased God through the folly of what we preach to save those who believe.' (1 Cor. 1:21) In the home this means of grace is imparted by family worship and devotions, and by parents instructing their children in the course of daily life (Deut. 6:4-6). In the church it happens through public preaching and teaching, and also through private discipleship and counseling (Acts 5:42).

Prayer. Married couples should pray together regularly, and teach their children how to commune with the Lord and intercede for others. The whole family should share this means of grace together, and public prayer is also one of the most important things a church can do. Remember, when Jesus condemned the Pharisees in Matthew 6, He was not condemning public prayer, but warning that private prayer should not be done in public in order to be seen by others. As for public prayer, Scripture encourages it: 'I desire then that in every place [church gatherings] the men should pray, lifting holy hands.' (1 Tim. 2:8)

Service. When a believer with a servant's heart assumes ministry responsibilities, he or she almost always benefits spiritually. The fact is, we often grow more in doing ministry than we do even from receiving ministry. So leaders in the home and the church should make sure that those under their care have opportunities to serve others.

Fellowship. Believers grow and unbelievers are brought to Christ when the people of God share fellowship together (Greek *koinonia*). This happens at worship services, small groups, meals, and other occasions where we share our love of Christ with one another by 'speaking the truth in love' (Eph. 4:15). On the other hand, when we don't spend time together we grow cold and ineffective, like a piece of charcoal in a grille that is removed from its companions and placed somewhere by itself. The coal will lose its warmth and glow, and will be useless until it is returned to the company of the others. Likewise, a good leader will ensure that his or her sheep flock together instead of separating themselves from one another.

Evangelism. Sharing the Gospel with others honors God and brings unparalleled joy into the life of the believer. When God uses us to bring others into the kingdom or to plant the seeds of the Gospel, it unleashes joy in our hearts that is almost inexplicable, and it also causes joy in heaven. As our Lord said: 'There is joy before the angels of God over one sinner who repents.' (Luke 15:10)

The sacraments. The Lord has given two sacraments to confirm the promises of the new covenant: baptism and the Lord's Supper. Baptism signifies the washing of forgiveness we have through the work of Christ, the believer's union with Him, and the trustworthiness of God's covenant promises. The Lord's Supper provides an opportunity for a regular focus on the Gospel truths of Christ's atoning death and triumphant resurrection, and by doing so encourages both personal renewal and church revival.

Those who neglect any or all of those means of grace are personally responsible before God for that serious spiritual problem. But many times their leaders will also be held accountable (Heb. 13:17), because they did not provide them with enough opportunities or encouragement.

> [A Christian leader] must manage his own household well, with all dignity, keeping his children submissive, for if someone does not know how to manage his own household, how will he care for God's church? (1 Tim. 3:4-5).

Three Leadership Styles

As Christian leaders are deployed to shepherd, serve, and superintend the people of God, they will each accomplish these dynamics through their own God-given personalities and gifts. They will need to lead in different ways at different times, so it would be helpful to consider the following three basic styles of leadership that we see taught or exemplified in the Scriptures.

Authoritative leadership

This style of leadership calls for direct orders to be given with clarity and the expectation of immediate compliance. Discussion and consensus is not needed. The authoritative style is appropriate during an emergency when time is critical and when a trusted leader is placed in command. It was the style of leadership practiced by the elders at the Miami-area church where our team volunteered following Hurricane Andrew. The church leadership had placed a Godly, capable, and trusted pastor in charge of a command post for helping the needy – and it was remarkably productive and efficient.

In a genuine emergency, decisive leadership is absolutely appropriate, but it's a short-term leadership style. If it's prolonged after the crisis has passed, it can produce resentment, confusion, and discouragement. Not only must there be a good reason for the use of an authoritative style, but trust in the leader is also essential for it to be successful.

Leaders who have consistently cared for their people and have demonstrated sustained character and accessibility can assume authoritative leadership when the occasion demands it. Those who have failed to do so will experience disaster if they attempt to lead in an authoritative style – no matter what the occasion might be. And even when used appropriately, the authoritative style should always be followed by a season of reorientation that will allow a renewal of the normal relationships between the leader and the people.

Participatory leadership

This approach is superior to the authoritative style, and is especially effective for longer term projects. It develops teamwork, educates the leader and participants, and builds respect and encouragement among them. By developing teamwork, participatory leadership helps reproduce and multiply leaders. By involving others in the tasks, it allows the leaders themselves to benefit from the knowledge, insights, and experience of other team members. Granted, too much information sharing can sometimes slow down problem solving and decision making, but a competent and responsible leader should be able to manage that challenge.

Participatory leadership builds up team leaders by depending upon them during the work and sharing the credit with them when it is completed. This is illustrated by the seemingly endless list of names of those who rebuilt the walls of Jerusalem, recorded in Nehemiah 3. Nehemiah knew that he could never have completed this project (in record time) without those other leaders mentioned, and he made sure that they could share in the glory. Such participatory leadership elevates morale for the task at hand and encourages excellence in future projects.

Delegated leadership

This style of leadership is the most effective for institutional settings and long-term situations. It both encourages 3D Leadership and is dependent on it. In fact, to successfully delegate responsibility, a leader must be constantly defining leadership, developing leaders, and deploying them in a biblical manner.

Delegation encourages individual team members to demonstrate ingenuity and initiative, which in turn helps develop new leaders. It must *not* become an excuse to dump distasteful tasks on others, but must be sincerely intended to define, develop, and deploy new leaders according to their unique gifts, passions, and abilities.

As I've said before, Christian leaders should never be 'lone rangers'. They should always be defining and developing leaders who can be deployed in their temporary or permanent absence, and this is best done by a team approach. This delegated style of leadership should be the norm within a church or other organization, and the established leaders should be habitually practicing it and improving in their implementation of it.[1]

Who is sufficient for these things? Not one of us. So it's time to pray:

> Dear Lord, please make me a watchful shepherd, give me a servant's heart, and sustain me as a diligent superintendent. Please, Lord, enable me to lead like Christ – the Good Shepherd, the Suffering Servant, and Vigilant Superintendent. May my leadership be marked by the ways of your Word and not by the ways of the world. Amen.

Prayer is the right place to start, but we must also put feet to our prayers by wading into the frontlines of spiritual warfare. The church needs to deploy leaders who are not fearful of the battle but are strong and courageous. We are well equipped with the armor of God, and our weapons are Divinely designed. In the next chapter we'll learn more about how to use them for the glory of God and the advancement of His kingdom.

---

1. See William A. Cohen, *The Art of the Leader* (Englewood Cliffs, NJ: Prentice Hall, 1990).

Questions for Thought and Discussion

1) Review the analogy of a shepherd discussed in this chapter, and consider it further. What makes someone a good or bad shepherd (in a literal sense), and what light does that shed on your work as a spiritual shepherd?

2) What kinds of thoughts might Satan have put in Jesus' mind to keep Him from washing the disciples' feet in John 13? How did Jesus overcome temptations like that, and how can all this help you in your leadership?

3) How are you practically and specifically providing the means of grace to those under your leadership? How can you improve?

4) How have you seen an authoritative leadership style used for good (by you or others) in your experience, and how have you seen it cause problems?

5) Pray the prayer at the end of the chapter, adding your own thoughts and words, and then pray in a similar way for at least one other leader or leader-in-training that you know.

Chapter 11

Fighting the Good Fight

IT'S a war.

Sometimes we forget that – but we shouldn't. Scripture repeatedly says that we Christians are engaged in ongoing spiritual warfare. That's another reason the church needs to abandon its fascination with the corporate models of leadership that the Bible never encourages. On the other hand, there are numerous biblical allusions, illustrations, and accounts of military leadership.

Scripture does not liken the church to a business, but it does describe it as the 'army of the LORD' (Josh. 5:14). In Ephesians 6:13-16, the members of the church are commanded to equip themselves with the 'armor of God' and to 'stand firm' with 'the belt of truth, and … the breastplate of righteousness'. 'In all circumstances,' the Apostle Paul adds in that passage, 'take up the shield of faith, with which you can extinguish all the flaming darts of the evil one; and take the helmet of salvation, and the sword of the Spirit, which is the word of God.' Satan's 'strongholds' are destroyed by 'the weapons of our warfare', according to 2 Corinthians 10:4. And in Psalm 144:1 we're told: 'Blessed be the LORD, my rock, who trains my hands for war, and my fingers for battle.'

We must never forget this essential biblical revelation: the church has an adversary, a powerful enemy called Satan, who heads a demonic army in this world. And we're engaged in mortal combat with him.

Think about it. If God's church is constantly engaged in spiritual warfare, then it is not a subset of the Christian life; it *is* the Christian life. Therefore, Christian leaders are really military leaders. They know we have an adversary who is seeking to destroy us, and they know we're under assault. Thankfully, victory in this war has already been ensured by the cross of Christ. The 'whole armor of God' is sufficient for the soldiers of Christ to stand firm, and the 'weapons of the Spirit' are powerfully designed by the Lord to take captive the minds and hearts of men and women. Even so, spiritual warfare – Christian combat – is the rule of the day until the Lord returns. In the army of the Lord there will be casualties, self-inflicted wounds, careless wounds, courageous warriors, martyrs for the Lord, and eventual victory.

Christian leaders should be taught what it means to follow the King into battle and lead his people 'from victory to victory'. Christian leaders must learn how to equip, inspire, and sustain the Lord's army. Our warfare is waged with spiritual weapons, but that does not make it any less a war. Christian leaders must teach others how to be 'soldiers of Christ', and how to lead them.

Do military metaphors and talk of war trouble you? If so, that's appropriate: spiritual warfare *is* troubling. Like physical war, it's an unfortunate result of the rebellion of Satan in heaven and the fall of man on earth. But that doesn't mean you should remain ignorant and unprepared – in fact the opposite is true. Inspired by the Holy Spirit on the eve of being called home to be with the Lord, Paul summarized his life's ministry in 2 Timothy 4:7 with a metaphor of war: 'I have fought the good fight, . . . I have kept the faith.'

When consistent with the truth of Scripture, instructions and illustrations from military leadership are appropriate and useful. So let's examine some in this chapter.

There are three types of leadership required for a victorious army: 1) visionary leadership, which gives direction; 2) strategic leadership, which develops a plan; and 3) tactical leadership, which implements the plan. Most leaders don't fit into only one of those categories – many are hybrids. The challenges at hand and the particular position of authority dictate the type of leadership that should be employed. Even so, most leaders are generally gifted in one type of leadership more than the others. Christian leadership is best advanced when leaders are trained to identify their own type of leadership (even if it is a hybrid) and then build teams of leaders that include all three types.

Visionary Leadership

When Imperial Japanese officers ended World War II with their official surrender in 1945, they did so aboard the battleship USS *Missouri* – Fleet Admiral Chester W. Nimitz's flagship. The *Missouri* was an appropriate location for the surrender ceremony because Nimitz had provided much of the vision for American victory in the Pacific. After the Japanese surprise attack on Pearl Harbor in 1941, he was named commander of the U.S. Pacific Fleet – at least what was left of it. His assignment: lead the U.S. Navy from a humiliating defeat and destroy the Japanese empire. Nimitz played a key role in developing the American vision for victory and was then given responsibility for executing much of it. At the battles of Coral Sea and Midway, he inflicted decisive defeats that stopped Japanese aggression and put the enemy on the defensive, which proved to be the turning point in the Pacific war. Never again would Imperial Japan hold so much of the world in its grasp.

Then, in joint operations with General Douglas MacArthur, Nimitz came up with a plan to steadily drive Japanese forces back across an immense range of the Pacific Ocean. Instead of trying to assault and capture every Japanese stronghold on countless islands dotting the Pacific – an effort that would have seriously slowed the American advance – Nimitz developed a vision of 'island hopping'. American forces bypassed nonessential Japanese strongholds, leaving them to be 'mopped up' later, and pressed forward to attack the Japanese mainland.

When the Japanese surrendered on V-J Day, no one had done more to earn the victory than Admiral Nimitz. Although strategically and tactically implemented by others, it was his vision that triumphed over the evil that had oppressed Asia and the Pacific.

Visionary leaders such as Admiral Nimitz understand a mission's objectives and how to organize a team to achieve the mission's goals.

They're able to visualize how the organization should function, what the team should do next, and what else needs to be accomplished. They have the ability to see the *end* from the *beginning* – and keep the vision alive so that the team can always see the prize ahead. They know that a strategic plan and its tactical execution are both crucial, so they strive to secure effective strategic and tactical leaders.

The importance of such visionary leadership is illustrated in the life of our Savior. Matthew 9:36-38 says: 'When he saw the crowds, he had compassion for them, because they were harassed and helpless, like sheep without a shepherd. Then he said to his disciples, "The harvest is plentiful, but the laborers are few; therefore pray earnestly to the Lord of the harvest to send out laborers into his harvest".' In Matthew 28:19-20 He tells His disciples: 'Go therefore and make disciples of all nations, baptizing them in the name of the Father and of the Son and of the Holy Spirit, teaching them to observe all that I have commanded you.' And in Acts 1:8 He adds: 'You will receive power when the Holy Spirit has come upon you, and you will be my witnesses in Jerusalem and in all Judea and Samaria, and to the end of the earth.' Our Lord's visionary leadership provided direction for the people who 'turned the world upside down' (Acts 17:6).

A visionary leader must first define the mission and then visualize its achievement. Then the necessary organization and execution can be achieved by strategic and tactical leaders who own the mission and the vision. For Christian leaders, of course, this must all be done in faithful obedience to the Word of God. It is the lamp to our feet and the light to our path (Ps. 119:105).

> Visionary leaders have the ability to see the *end* from the *beginning* – and keep the vision alive so that the team can always see the prize ahead.

Strategic Leadership

A strategic leader embraces a vision, develops a plan for achieving the vision's goals, and ensures that the tactical leaders implement it successfully with an economy of resources.

Visionary leaders tend to be immediately passionate about the vision, and eager to share it. But they may not have a strategic plan for implementing the vision, and most choose to delegate that crucial task to a strategic leader. The strategic leader then creates an effective pathway to victory and develops the organizational structure required, including a system to utilize and respond to any criticism of the plan.

A classic example of strategic leadership occurred during the American War for Independence at an obscure meadow in the Carolina backcountry, and led directly to our American nationhood. General George Washington's vision for victory in the American Revolution appeared dim in late 1780. Although American militia troops had won a key victory at the battle of King's Mountain in the South and long-awaited French reinforcements had arrived in the North, British forces had scored a series of victories and the American cause remained in peril.

Washington's army was stalemated in New Jersey, some of his troops had mutinied over lack of pay, and one of his most valued officers – General Benedict Arnold – had deserted to the enemy. British troops still occupied New York City, had resisted an attempted American advance onto Staten Island, and were mounting an aggressive Southern campaign in the Carolinas. In one of the worst American disasters of the war, the key port city of Charleston, South Carolina had fallen to the British. Savannah, Georgia was also in British hands, and a British army had inflicted a costly and humiliating defeat on American troops at the battle of Camden.

The American cause desperately needed a victory to reverse the direction of the war – and it happened in the South Carolina backwoods, thanks to the strategic leadership of an American brigadier general named Daniel Morgan. Morgan was an experienced Continental officer serving under the brilliant General Nathanael Greene, and was charged with helping turn back the British campaign to capture and occupy the Carolinas. In January 1781, Morgan's outnumbered army was hemmed in between a flooded, impassable river and a crack British army led by a ruthless and tempestuous commander named Banastre

Tarleton. Yet Morgan's perilous position was by choice – it was actually a trap he planned to spring on the British. He knew that Lieutenant Colonel Tarleton favored rash frontal assaults, and he had intentionally deployed his troops to lure the British into combat.

Morgan had strategically selected the field of battle with which I am familiar and upon which I have walked many times – a sprawling, tree-lined pasture known as the Cowpens – and he intended to unleash a secret strategy on the British. The night before the battle, Morgan moved among the camps of his small army, making speeches to his soldiers and encouraging them to do their best in the pending combat. When he finished, according to an eyewitness, his troops were 'in good spirits and very willing to fight'.[1]

When the British attacked the next day, on the bitterly cold morning of January 17, 1781, Morgan had his army deployed in three lines: experienced and well-trained Continental regulars in the rear, volunteer militia troops in the center, and a force of hidden sharpshooters in the front. When the British came into range, marching forward in the frontal assault as Morgan had predicted, he gave an order and the sharpshooters opened fire on the British officers, eliminating much of their leadership. The second line of militia, which had a reputation for firing a single volley and then fleeing, had promised Morgan that they would stand firm and fire two volleys before retreating.

They did, and the British army charged after them – right into a surprise cavalry assault from their flanks. The well-trained British infantry took their losses and kept coming, but then saw the militia and the Continental regulars in front of them turn and appear to flee. Without officers to control them, the British troops broke ranks and made an undisciplined charge. At Morgan's order, the American troops suddenly stopped their retreat, turned, and fired volley after volley into the surprised British troops – and then followed up with a bold bayonet charge. The shock attack was

---

1. William Seymour, 'Journal of the Southern Expedition, 1780–1783,' *Pennsylvania Magazine of History and Biography,* 1883, 7:294.

too much for the British, who had few officers left to rally them, and their army was routed.

The battle of Cowpens (the basis for the climactic battle in the movie *The Patriot*) was an overwhelming American victory, and came at a crucial time in the War for Independence. It launched a series of military successes in the South that eventually led to the British surrender at Yorktown and American independence – due in large part to the strategic leadership of Brigadier General Daniel Morgan. It was Washington's vision to defeat the British in the South, but it was Morgan's strategy that made it happen in reality. The commander-in-chief was far away in New Jersey when Morgan's victory occurred in South Carolina.

> Strategic leaders create an effective pathway to victory and develop the organizational structure required, including a system to utilize and respond to any criticism of the plan.

Tactical Leadership

Visionary and strategic leadership are essential, but no battle is won by them alone. It's won by the soldier, and the soldier wins it with tactics: the methods and means of executing a strategic plan. That requires a tactical leader.

Major General John A. Lejeune, a U.S. Marine Corps officer in World War I, provides us with a superb example of tactical leadership. In the autumn of 1918, Allied forces – bolstered by the American Expeditionary Force – launched an offensive to drive German forces from the western front in France and Belgium. At the center of the advance in the French region of Champagne, French troops stalled against a powerful German stronghold called Blanc Mont Ridge, and the French commander turned to General Lejeune for assistance. Lejeune commanded the U.S. Second Division, a hard-fighting unit of both army and marine troops.

A mixture of army soldiers and marines in a single division might have proved troublesome to some commanders, but not to Lejeune, whose leadership had shaped the division into a highly regarded combat unit. At Blanc Mont Ridge, the French high command wanted to break up the Second Division and spread its men throughout the battle-weary French forces, which would have placed the Americans directly under French officers and would have eliminated the division's identity. Lejeune was outranked, but he adamantly urged his superiors not to break up his division – he said his men knew how to take Blanc Mont Ridge, and they would do it.

Reluctantly, the Allied commanders agreed to let him try. And the American troops of the Second Division launched a mighty assault on the German stronghold on October 3, 1918. It was a bloody, two-hour uphill battle. Amid the fierce fighting, the supporting French troops faltered on both American flanks, causing Lejeune's men to draw blistering enemy machine-gun fire from both sides. They persevered, however, capturing the ridge and holding it until they were finally reinforced. The Second Division assault on Blanc Mont Ridge spearheaded a sustained American drive that significantly contributed to the Allied victory in World War I.

The French were so impressed that they awarded 2,000 Croix de Guerre medals to Lejeune's men, and presented Lejeune himself with the Legion of Honor. Back home, he was awarded the American Distinguished Service Cross and was promoted to commandant of the U.S. Marine Corps. Today, the Marine Corps' huge base in coastal North Carolina is named Camp Lejeune in his honor.

Tactical leaders embrace the vision from the visionary leader and the strategy from the strategic leader, and then provide the necessary leadership to equip, empower, and execute the plan by taking it from the paper to the battlefield. They understand the training and organization needed, for example, and the deadlines that must be met. They also know the strengths and weaknesses of their people. They can predict obstacles and establish contingency plans, so that those who are engaged in the effort will be able to adapt and overcome. Any strategic plan can be interrupted by an emergency, falter because of poor communications, or be derailed by uncontrollable events. Therefore, all armies need leaders who have the 'on-site' skills like flexibility and decisiveness that are needed for successful tactical leadership.

> Tactical leaders predict obstacles and establish contingency plans, so that those who are engaged in the effort will be able to adapt and overcome.

Spiritual Warfare Leadership and You

As I said earlier, leaders seldom fit perfectly into only one of these types of leadership. When assembling a team, the primary oversight should always be given to someone who generally meets the definition of a visionary leader and can provide direction. But this doesn't necessarily mean that team meetings should be led by a visionary. Some visionary leaders are not skillful discussion leaders, and in some cases organizational sessions are most effectively directed by the strategic leader. Sometimes the strategic leader focuses on developing a plan, and leaves the execution to one tactical leader. But sometimes a team has numerous tactical leaders, who each hold responsibility for some part of the execution, which in turn advances strategy and implements the vision. The exact roles chosen for each leader will depend on the particular situation and personnel, of course, but a general guideline is that we should try to match the type of leadership needed with the leader whose gifts and experience fit best with that type.

The complementary roles played by the Apostles in the early church's task of reaching the world outside of Israel is an illustration of different types of leadership. Peter was a visionary leader, who responded to God's call by 'opening the kingdom' to the Gentiles at the house of Cornelius and reporting back to the other leaders in Jerusalem (Acts 10). James acted as a strategic leader when he led the Jerusalem Council to remove barriers that would keep the Gentiles from converting to the faith (Acts 15). And Philip was a tactical leader who implemented the 'world vision' by starting his ministry in neighboring Samaria, and then evangelizing an Ethiopian eunuch who was headed back to Africa and could take the Gospel there with him (Acts 8). The Apostle Paul, on the other hand, was clearly a hybrid who was skilled at all three types of leadership. He was a great visionary who promoted the big idea of world evangelization (Rom. 15:9-12), an effective strategist who developed a plan to systematically reach new areas (Rom. 15:19-20), and a brilliant tactician who adjusted to the challenges and opportunities that arose during his mission (Rom. 15:22-28).

Whether you are a visionary, strategic, or tactical leader, or a combination of those types, remember that you should never ask those you lead to do something that you're not willing to do yourself.

Soon after the armistice that ended World War I on November 11, 1918, General Lejeune visited some of his wounded troops in a field hospital. One was a Marine Corps sergeant who had been severely wounded in an assault on a bridge in the fading hours of the war. Here's how Lejeune himself recalled the ultimate lesson in leadership that was illustrated by the wounded combat veteran:

> I asked him if he had heard before the battle that the Armistice would probably be signed within a few hours. He replied that it was a matter of common knowledge among the men. I then said, 'What induced you to cross the bridge in the face of that terrible machine gun and artillery fire when you expected that the war would end in a few hours?' In answer, he said, 'Just before we began to cross the bridge our battalion commander, Captain Dunbeck, assembled the companies around him in the ravine where we were waiting orders, and told us, "Men, I am going across that river, and I expect you to go with me".' The wounded man then remarked, 'What could we do but go across too? Surely we couldn't let him go by himself; we love him too much for that.' I have always felt that the incident I have just narrated gives one a better understanding of the meaning and the practice of leadership than do all the books that have been written, and all the speeches that have been made on the subject.[2]

You too can be a selfless leader who inspires your followers, by going anywhere and doing anything that you expect of them. It's not just military tradition. It's the biblical model of leadership. Did not our Savior take the high ground before calling us into the battle? Our Savior went to the cross and met the judgment of God due to us to save us from our sins and then met and defeated all

---

2. John A. Lejeune, *The Reminiscences of a Marine* (Philadelphia: Dorrance and Company, 1930), p. 383.

of our enemies – not only sin but Satan, death, Hell and the grave. He now beckons us to follow Him; therefore we gladly follow into battle the Savior who loves us and did much to save us, not to make much of us but to set us free to make much of Him. We follow Him because we love Him who first loved us – *'Lead on O King Eternal until sins fierce war shall cease.'*

As a Christian leader you will always be in a spiritual war, and you face a powerful adversary. But also remember this: you are not alone. The battle is the Lord's, and you have been called into the battle for the Lord. If in your heart you commit to *defining, developing,* and *deploying* leaders while seeking to be a leader who is faithful and effective yourself, Satan will assuredly attack. The last thing that he wants to see happen is the church becoming a leadership factory and distribution center that fills the world with Godly Christian leaders. So what does he do to prevent that? We'll learn more about his plan, and how to defeat him, in the next chapter.

Questions for Thought and Discussion

1) What would you say to someone who objects to the use of historical military illustrations in Bible teaching, because war is such a horrible thing?

2) What are some good and bad examples of visionary leadership, and what can you learn from them?

3) What principles of strategic leadership can you see in the Battle of Cowpens described in this chapter (or in the movie *The Patriot*), and what can you learn from them?

4) Why was it so important for General Lejeune to keep his troops together at the Battle of Blanc Mont Ridge in World War 1, and what applications can be made from that to your spiritual leadership?

5) Are you most gifted and experienced at visionary, strategic, or tactical leadership (or a combination)? Take some time to pray for further understanding and usefulness in the kind(s) of leadership to which God is calling you.

Chapter 12

Know Your Enemy

SATAN is defeated. But still he 'prowls around like a roaring lion, seeking someone to devour' (1 Pet. 5:8). He's like the Germans after D-Day in World War II: the Allies' victory was inevitable after that successful invasion, but the Nazis still caused a lot of death and destruction before their final surrender almost a year later.

Jesus Christ won the decisive battle when He entered this world two thousand years ago. As 1 John 3:8 says: 'The reason the Son of God appeared was to destroy the works of the devil.' He was victorious over Satan, whose preordained future lies in the lake of fire. But for the present the devil remains 'the prince of the power of the air, the spirit that is now at work in the sons of disobedience' (Eph. 2:2), and we Christians are engaged in warfare with him and his allies. Every Christian needs to know and obey God's directions to put on the 'whole armor of God' as directed in Ephesians 6:10-18, and this is especially true of leaders because the enemy targets them specifically. But by the power of God – not on your own – you *can* thwart his spiritual attacks, regardless of how difficult the circumstances may be.

Let's remember one thing right up front: spiritual warfare is not a battle between gods. Satan is not the bad god and Yahweh the good god. There is only one God. Satan is a wannabe – a fallen angel of high rank created by God, but one that is now under Divine judgment forever. Ultimately, in His perfect timing, God will end the days of Satan by casting him into the lake of fire (Rev. 20:10).

In the meantime, we must remember these two essential truths about spiritual warfare: First, Satan is defeated and awaiting his ultimate demise. As we sing in Martin Luther's great hymn, 'A Mighty Fortress Is Our God', 'One little word shall fell him.' That will occur according to God's timing, not the enemy's. Second, we are called to put on our armor and 'fight the good fight' (1 Tim. 6:12). We don't have to do it alone because we've been given the Spirit of God, and 'he who is in you is greater than he who is in the world' (1 John 4:4). And thankfully the Spirit has already revealed Satan's assault plan to us. It's all in the Word of God, and by the grace of God we can know it and apply it.

The great heavyweight fighter, Joe Louis, was once asked how he disposed of his opponents so quickly. Reportedly, he replied that he knew them well enough to know what they were going to do before they even knew what they were going to do. Fortunately for us, we can have that kind of knowledge regarding Satan. You can know what your spiritual opponent is going to do before he even knows, because God's Word tells us all about our adversary. Let's learn about his strategies and snares, so as a Christian leader you can be prepared for the attacks that will inevitably come.

Satan's Strategies

Satan hates what God loves, and since God loves His people, Satan will seek to destroy the church. Broadly speaking, his basic strategies are persecution and penetration, which are proliferated through the many allies he has recruited.

Persecution

Satan's first strategy is to use 'the world' (Greek *cosmos*) – the earthly system of rebellion of which he is the ruler – to bring persecution against the church of Jesus Christ. He does that by focusing on individual Christian leaders and the church as a whole. It's spiritual warfare, but sometimes he uses evil governments and tyrannical leaders who knowingly or unknowingly follow him.

Satan's minions – the evil tyrants of history – never seem to learn what will happen to them for persecuting God's beloved until it's too late. They ultimately suffer the devastating end predicted in

Psalm 14:4-5: 'Have they no knowledge, all the evildoers who eat up my people as they eat bread and do not call upon the LORD? There they are in great terror, for God is with the generation of the righteous.' And by the grace of the Sovereign God, Satan's persecution of believers inevitably becomes an instrument for the growth of the church.

In the book of Acts, for instance, the church was persecuted in Jerusalem, and then multiplied in Judea and Samaria (Acts 7-8). The Roman government then martyred tens of thousands of Christians, but their faith ended up conquering the entire Empire within several hundred years. When an atheistic communist regime seized power in China after World War II, there were probably 80,000 Christians in that nation, and China's communist leaders tried to eliminate them all by incarceration and execution. Today, however, there are an estimated 100 million Christians in China. Likewise, a series of tyrannical leaders in East Africa have been intent on destroying the believers under their despotic regimes, but God sent a revival to that region. The result is a thriving church with millions of members, whose leaders are so strong that many in America now look to them for inspiration and direction.

Penetration

This strategy of Satan is less obvious than persecution, but even more insidious: he seeks to destroy the church from within. It's an old strategy that was happening even in the time of the Apostle Paul, who warned the elders at Ephesus about it. 'I know that after my departure,' he says in Acts 20:29, 'fierce wolves will come in *among you* [the leaders of the church], not sparing the flock.' Old and exposed as it is, however, Satan's penetration plan can still do immense damage, often because those under attack don't recognize the assault. It's a two-pronged attack: penetration in the fellowship and penetration in the leadership.

When Satan penetrates the fellowship, he will often attempt to distract, delay, and eventually destroy the work of the local church through a rising cacophony of grumbling and complaints. And he will also attempt to penetrate the ranks of leaders to discourage and eventually destroy their ministry by placing 'fierce wolves' – false teachers – inside the leadership and by luring legitimate leaders into sin. Leaders must resist both attacks by knowing the Word of God, applying it, and calling upon the Lord consistently in prayer.

Remember, Satan targets leaders in particular with his assault strategies. Yet the Bible does not tell the believer or the leader to flee, but to resist Satan and *he* will flee (James 4:7).

Proliferation

According to Scripture, Satan doesn't wage warfare against God and the saints just by himself, but has filled the world with many allies who do his bidding.

First are the fallen angels who were cast out of heaven with him under the judgment of God, according to Revelation 12:7-9. While Satan does not have God's omnipresent nature, he is apparently ubiquitous. In other words, he is not everywhere all the time, but he *can* be anywhere at any time. And his influence is also expanded by the dispersal of his demonic force of spiritual principalities and authorities who have the same ability. While the exact number of demons is not stated in Scripture, it must be significantly large if hundreds can be devoted to one individual person, as revealed in the story of the demoniac named 'Legion' (Mark 5:1-13).

The second company of Satan's allies are the unbelieving educators, entertainers, entrepreneurs, etc., that are being influenced by demonic powers to aid in creating the evil system that the Bible calls 'the world'. Jesus was referring to that system when He told His disciples: 'Because you are not of the world, but I chose you out of the world, therefore the world hates you.' (John 15:19; cf. John 17) Satan is called 'the ruler of this world' (John 16:11) and 'the god of this world' (1 Cor. 4:4), and unbelievers are said to be living by 'the spirit of the world' and 'the wisdom of the world' (1 Cor. 2:12; 3:19). So the people that are most influential in the earthly cultures where Christ is denied, even though they may not be aware of it, are agents of Satan in the sense that they are promoting his ideas, values, priorities, and goals through their influence. As James 4:4 says: 'Whoever wishes to be a friend of the world makes himself an enemy of God,' and therefore has become an ally of Satan.

Satan's third group of allies consists of the numerous 'antichrists' who have arisen throughout the ages and litter the pages of history – tyrants who have either intentionally or ignorantly served the devil in their lust for power and possessions. The Apostle John says in 1 John 2:18 that 'many antichrists have come', and in 2 Thessalonians 2:3-4 Paul speaks about a 'man of lawlessness ... the son of destruction' who has often been associated with the beast in Revelation and referred to as '*the* Antichrist'. Christians may differ on exactly whom those passages are about, but it should be clear to all that Satan often empowers and allies himself with government leaders who defy God, despise His people, and deceive the world.

> You can know what your spiritual opponent is going to do before he even knows, because God's Word tells us all about our adversary.

Satan's Snares

As the enemy of our souls implements his strategies of persecution, penetration, and proliferation, he does so with specific tactics that the Bible calls 'snares' (1 Tim. 3:7; 2 Tim. 2:26). The best way to avoid falling into a trap is to know it is there ahead of time, so we need to take some time to consider the ways that Satan and his minions will try to ensnare your soul, and therefore limit or destroy your effectiveness as a Christian leader.

Temptations to lust and boast

'For all that is in the world, the lust of the flesh and the lust of the eyes and boastful pride of life, is not from the Father, but is from the world.' (1 John 2:16, NASB) Satan has always and will always use these three temptations to trap believers in general and leaders in particular. He uses 'the lust of the flesh' – an inordinate desire for physical pleasure – to draw us away from the Lord. He uses 'the lust of the eyes', which is a longing to have more than God has seen fit to give us. And he uses 'the boastful pride of life' to make us want things like importance and acceptance more than we want to please Him.

In the garden Adam and Eve fell into all three of these traps. Genesis 3:6 says that 'when the woman saw that the tree was good for food [the lust of the flesh], and that it was a delight to the eyes [the lust of the eyes], and that the tree was to be desired to make one wise [the boastful pride of life], she took from its fruit and she ate.'

Satan not only used this threefold scheme on the first Adam, he attempted to do the same to the second Adam, Jesus Christ, though this time it was in a wilderness instead of a garden. First, Satan appealed to the lust of the flesh, trying to take advantage of Jesus' hunger. 'If you are the Son of God,' he taunted, 'command these stones to become loaves of bread.' (Matt. 4:3) Jesus resisted the temptation and responded with the Word of God: 'It is written: "Man shall not live by bread alone, but by every word that comes from the mouth of God".' (Matt. 4:4, quoting Deut. 8:3) He affirmed the sufficiency of God and the priority of the spiritual over the physical, and that's what those who bear His name must do when Satan attacks us with the lust of the flesh. Respond with the Word, and put the spiritual above the physical.

As he continued his temptation of the Lord, Satan next appealed to the lust of the eyes, visually offering the crown jewels from his temporary domain – what Luke 4:5 refers to as 'all the kingdoms of the world'. In exchange, the devil asked for what he's always wanted: 'If you, then, will worship me, it will all be yours.' (Luke 4:7) Setting the model for us, Jesus again defeated the temptation by quoting the Word: 'It is written, "You shall worship the Lord your God, and Him only shall you serve".' (Luke 4:8, quoting Deut. 6:13) Be careful when you find yourself thinking too much about 'nickels and noses' in your ministry, and when you are tempted to be discontent in any other way through what you see around you.

In his third and final effort to tempt Jesus, Satan attacked with an appeal to the boastful pride of life, trying to draw Christ into the trap of arrogance and make him derail his ministry mission in a demonstration of power and influence at the pinnacle of the temple. 'If you are the Son of God, throw yourself down from here, for it is written, "He will command his angels concerning you, to guard you," and "On their hands they will bear you up, lest you strike your foot against a stone".' (Luke 4:9-11, quoting Ps. 91:11, 12) Again

Jesus fought the temptation with the Word of God: 'It is written, "You shall not put the Lord your God to the test".' Our Lord humbly gave glory to God the Father rather than to Himself, and so should you when you are tempted to be angered by criticism or puffed up by compliments.

Satan fled when it was apparent that none of these traps would work on Jesus, and he will do the same when we resist him (James 4:7).

Remember, God designs tests so that we will grow. Satan designs temptations to destroy us. At times, Satan will attempt to use God's tests as temptations as he did with Adam and Eve. God had called them to the test of obedience in subduing the earth, ruling the creatures, and being fruitful and multiplying while refraining from eating from the tree of the knowledge of good and evil. Satan turned that test into a temptation. But also know that God can use Satan's temptations as His tests in order to grow us, as He did with Peter. Peter was tempted by Satan to deny the Lord, but God turned the temptation into a test designed to grow him through brokenness and the gracious gifts of confession and repentance.

So how should we live in light of these snares of Satan? Flee temptation. Daily kill the 'old man'. Trust God in the tests of life. Surrender to the power of the Spirit of God. Know and use the Word of God as you put on the armor of God. Stay focused upon the glory of God, with prayerful reliance upon the grace of God as you use the weapons of God to advance the kingdom of God. Finally, remember our Lord's words to His disciples as the evil one came for him through the betrayal of Judas: 'Watch and pray that you may not enter into temptation. The spirit is indeed willing, but the flesh is weak' (Matt. 26:41).

Addictions to power, sex, and money

We are all addicts by nature, in the sense that we were created to worship God habitually, and when we don't, that hole will inevitably be filled by something else. So as creatures of habit who are built to worship, we can easily be enslaved by false gods.

Addiction to power can become one of them, because power corrupts, and Satan knows that as well as anyone. That's why so many Christian leaders default to controlling people instead of serving them. Beware, leader! You are called to be a servant, not a lord. Which are you? Ask yourself that question early and often, build relationships with others who will ask you that question regularly, and always answer it with judgment day honesty before the Lord. As a leader, you must make sure that you're held accountable to others in authority over you, then humbly listen to their advice. Practice accountability and submission!

Addiction to sex has always been one of Satan's most powerful weapons (consider all the examples in the Old Testament), and it is one of his favorites still today. Satan loves to use our culture's preoccupation with immorality. America is drowning in a cesspool of sexual preoccupation, promiscuity, and perversion – all of which are shamelessly promoted by our mass media. To remain oblivious to this is to court disaster.

Almost daily, it seems, Christian leaders fall into this particular trap of Satan. As a Christian leader you must seek accountability from trustworthy colleagues and be open to intentional inquiry by others to assist you in avoiding this snare. One prominent Christian leader managed to stay above reproach in this area for a lifetime of integrity by establishing safeguards early in his ministry that some may have considered extreme. He never allowed himself to be alone with someone of the opposite sex. Office doors were always left open. His wife or an associate was always present in counseling sessions or meetings with women. He recruited a select group of associates that were always ready to hold him accountable, and he voluntarily placed himself under the authority of a supervisory board of leaders. My advice to every leader is: 'Go thou and do likewise!'

Addiction to money is another age-old and always powerful tool in Satan's arsenal. The love of money has corrupted many ministries and disqualified untold numbers of leaders. There's a reason that the Lord said, 'No one can serve two masters, for either he will hate the one and love the other, or he will be devoted to the one and despise the other. You cannot serve God and money.' (Matt. 6:24) That's why Proverbs 30:8 suggests this prayer: 'Give me neither poverty nor riches; feed me with the food that is needful for me, lest I be full and deny you and say, "Who is the Lord?" or lest I be poor and steal and profane the name of my God.' You can have very little wealth and a meager income but still be addicted to money.

A Christian's lifestyle should be arranged to honor the supremacy of Christ rather than 'the love of money,' which is 'a root of all kinds of evils' (1 Tim. 6:10). Christian leaders especially should be transparent and accountable to recognized authorities in both their personal and ministry financial stewardship. A Christian leader or a ministry should never have cause to be ashamed when their financial records are revealed. As one Christian business leader, who is highly respected in our community, said, 'Pastor, in life, the Christian should always do the next right thing for the Lord.' And it is always right to practice integrity in our financial conduct.

> Satan fled when it was apparent that none of his traps would work on Jesus, and he will do the same when we resist him (James 4:7).

Capitulations to fear, frustration, and fatigue

Power, sex, and money might be the 'big three' temptations for Christian leaders, but in my experience another three are not far behind in their destructive capabilities. Christians in general, and leaders in particular, become especially vulnerable to Satan's schemes when caught in one of these snares: fear, frustration, or fatigue.

'The fear of man lays a snare,' according to Proverbs 29:25. When we allow ourselves to be unduly afraid, we're more susceptible to Satan's lies and deceit. Step back, call on the Lord, plunge into the Word, and turn away from fear. 'The Lord is my helper; I will not fear; what can man do to me?' (Heb. 13:6, quoting Ps. 118:6)

What's the best defense against fear? It's more than mere personal courage or resolve – it's love. First John 4:18 says that 'perfect love casts out all fear'. The only perfect love in existence is God's love, and its greatest display is the love of Christ on the cross. 'We love because he first loved us.' (1 John 4:19) So grow in your love for Him by remembering the Gospel, learning His Word, immersing yourself in prayer, and committing to other biblical priorities in your life and ministry leadership. You cannot be delivered from Satan's snares on your own, but God can easily do it for you in a moment. So don't look to yourself, your talents, your gifts, or your self-confidence; in other words, 'put no confidence in the flesh' (Phil. 3:3), and remember that 'it is the spirit who gives life' (John 6:63; 2 Cor. 3:6). Call on the Lord and trust fully in the unfailing love of Christ.

Frustration also makes us vulnerable to Satan's schemes, and we easily become frustrated when we take on too much. Inspired by the Holy Spirit, Paul declared: 'One thing I do.' (Phil. 3:13) The more our culture embraces complexity, multitasking, and over-loading, the more the church should be encouraging simplicity in life. Christian leaders, like others, need margins in their work (times for rest and reflection) as well as margins in their finances (sacrificial giving and limits on spending). Take charge of simplifying your workload and lifestyle, or engage someone else to help you do it. Planning is appropriate since we are made in the image of God, but it also reminds us that our planning should be God-centered, and when God redirects our plan we are to respond with contentment and trust. As Proverbs 16:9 says: 'The heart of a man plans his way, but the LORD establishes his steps.' So learn to rest in the sovereignty of God, especially for your work and finances, as He establishes your steps and causes all things to 'work together for good, for those who are called according to his purpose' (Rom. 8:28).

Finally, avoid fatigue. It's like a sharpener for Satan's sword. Sometimes fatigue is a legitimate result of being 'poured out as a drink offering' (2 Tim. 4:6), but often it's unnecessarily self-imposed.

One of the ways you can escape this snare of Satan is to enjoy the benefits of the Sabbath principle. It is God's gift to us – even though many believers and leaders fail to fully embrace it. 'The Sabbath was made for man,' said the Lord, 'not man for the Sabbath' (Mark 2:27). The early Christians made full use of synagogue worship on Saturday for evangelism, but they intentionally turned to assemble as believers for worship on the Lord's Day, commemorating the resurrection of Christ. Thus they maintained the Sabbath principle – worship and rest one day in seven. I suggest you do the same: use the Lord's Day as it is designed for the purpose of physical rest and renewal, time alone with God and with your family, and the gathering of God's people for public worship to declare the majesty of our Triune God. The proper use of God's gift of the Sabbath can change your life and provide protection from all of Satan's snares.

Those three vulnerabilities – fear, frustration, and fatigue – are often connected. When you become fearful, you don't sleep well, which makes you frustrated, and eventually the two pile on to make you fatigued. Then you're on edge, tense, easily provoked, lacking in judgment, devoid of patience – and you become an enticing target for Satan. So decide now to thwart Satan's use of fear, frustration, and fatigue. Plan for appropriate physical exercise, rest, and regular spiritual renewal. Then you can practice leadership efficiently – functioning physically, mentally, emotionally, and spiritually through a daily trust in the sufficiency of Christ, and living out that trust with wisdom and the full use of the means of grace in your life.

Summarizing the Schemes and Snares of Satan

The book of Acts bears witness and church history illustrates that whenever the kingdom of God advances throughout the world the 'evil empire' of Satan will strike back. The schemes and snares that Satan uses can be summarized in this way: *intimidation, infiltration* and *imitation*.

Satan tries to stop the advancement of the Gospel of the kingdom first through *intimidation*. By persecution from the culture or the state, he attempts to silence the church through intimidating the leadership and/or the fellowship.

Secondly, he attempts to thwart the progress of the Gospel of the kingdom through *infiltration*. He infiltrates the followership by promoting schism, division, gossip, slander, etc. He tries to infiltrate the leadership as he did the elders at Ephesus, with false teachers who pervert the Scriptures or false leaders who 'draw away the disciples after them' (Acts 20:28-30).

Thirdly, he attempts to deter the progress of the Gospel of the kingdom through *imitation* by promoting false religions – even many that call themselves 'Christian'. Jesus referred to such false professions of Christianity as 'the tares of the field' that would be sown among the wheat (Matt. 13:24-30). Satan is the one who sows the tares, in order to undermine the witness of Christianity and deceive seekers to a false religion. A prime example is the theological liberalism that masquerades as 'mainline Christianity' deceptively using the same vocabulary as biblical Christianity when in reality it is absolutely antithetical to it.

> Inspired by the Holy Spirit, Paul declared, 'One thing I do.' (Phil. 3:13) The more our culture embraces complexity, multi-tasking, and overloading, the more the church should be encouraging simplicity in life.

Standing up to Satan

The Apostle Paul summarizes our part in spiritual warfare well in 1 Corinthians 10:31: 'So, whether you eat or drink, or whatever you do, do it all to the glory of God.' We should not live to eat; we should eat to live for Christ. We should not live to drink; we should drink to live for Christ. Satan tried to defeat Jesus by the lust of the flesh, the lust of the eyes, and the boastful pride of life. Instead, Christ defeated Satan by the Holy Spirit and the Word of God.

As Christian leaders, we must know the enemy and deal with him biblically, and remember that Jesus Christ is victorious. So while you must flee temptation, you must not flee Satan. Instead, as Scripture instructs, resist him: 'Submit yourselves therefore to God. Resist the devil, and he will flee from you.' (James 4:7) Flee temptation. Resist Satan. Then he will flee from you. But remember, your confidence should not be in yourself: it's the Lord who deals with Satan on your behalf. 'The horse is made ready for the day of battle, but the victory belongs to the Lord.' (Prov. 21:31)

Always remember these three marvelous Gospel truths: First, Jesus defeated Satan and all the principalities and powers of evil at the cross. Jesus made a mockery of the kingdom of darkness and held it up for ridicule. He bound the strong man (Mark 3:27).

Granted, God has allowed the devil a lengthy chain for the moment, but he *is* defeated: '[Jesus] disarmed the rulers and authorities and put them to open shame, by triumphing over them.' (Col. 2:15) Second, the Bible reveals that the Holy Spirit lives within you. And the Holy Spirit of God is infinitely more powerful than Satan: 'Little children, you are from God and have overcome them, for he who is in you is greater than he who is in the world.' (1 John 4:4) Third, Scripture also reveals that Jesus Christ, the Lord of lords and King of kings, is continually interceding for you at the throne of God the Father in the magnificent, unfathomable fellowship of God's triune glory.

That ministry of Christ for you, and the conquering love that motivates it, is triumphantly proclaimed in Romans 8:33-39:

> Who shall bring any charge against God's elect? It is God who justifies. Who is to condemn? Christ Jesus is the one who died – more than that, who was raised – who is at the right hand of God, who indeed is interceding for us. Who shall separate us from the love of Christ? Shall tribulation, or distress, or persecution, or famine, or nakedness, or danger, or sword? As it is written, 'For your sake we are being killed all day long; we are regarded as sheep to be slaughtered.' No, in all these things we are more than conquerors through Him who loved us. For I am sure that neither death nor life, nor angels nor rulers, nor things present nor things to come, nor powers, nor height nor depth, nor anything else in all creation, will be able to separate us from the love of God in Christ Jesus our Lord.

Spiritual warfare is a reality of the Christian walk, but you can stand firm as a leader in the Lord. Show those under your care how to be equipped with the whole armor of God and 'take every thought captive to obey Christ' (2 Cor. 10:5). Be a leader who reproduces and multiplies yourself as you make Gospel-driven and Christ-centered disciples. And always make sure that those whom you disciple are not ignorant of Satan's schemes. Your marching orders as a Christian leader are plainly stated in 2 Timothy 4:1-5:

> I charge you in the presence of God and of Christ Jesus, who is to judge the living and the dead, and by his appearing and his kingdom: preach the word; be ready in season and out of season; reprove, rebuke, and exhort, with complete patience and teaching. For the

time is coming when people will not endure sound teaching, but having itching ears they will accumulate for themselves teachers to suit their own passions, and will turn away from listening to the truth and wander off into myths. As for you, always be sober-minded, endure suffering, do the work of an evangelist, fulfill your ministry.

Define new leaders
Develop them
Deploy them.

Re-establish the church as a leadership factory and distribution center. And by God's grace we may hear again, 'These men who have turned the world upside down have come here also.' (Acts 17:6) What glorious days lie ahead and what exciting opportunities are before us, as we unleash Christian leaders who will be world-shakers. Those kinds of leaders not only 'turn the world upside down', but they also *turn it right side up* as the Gospel of Jesus Christ is proclaimed and lived in thought, word, and deed. The enemies of God become the people of God. Lives that are in disarray are redeemed, families are reclaimed, and a culture is transformed.

O God, do it again and begin with me.

Questions for Thought and Discussion

1) Why is it worth taking a whole chapter in a book about leadership to learn about your enemy/opponent? Consider analogies from military and sports leadership.

2) Think more about the evil system called 'the world' discussed in this chapter, which according to 1 John 5:19 'lies in the power of the evil one.' What are some examples of people 'selling their souls to the devil' in some way and succeeding in the world? Read Psalm 73 to learn more about this, and especially what David says about 'their end'.

3) What temptations (or 'snares of Satan') cause you the most trouble? Take some time to consider carefully and thoroughly how he seeks to ensnare you in those ways. For the purpose of being better prepared to resist him, imagine the specifics of how he might be tempting you, like C. S. Lewis does in *The Screwtape Letters*.

4) By discussing fear, frustration, and fatigue along with the 'big three' of power, sex, and money, this chapter implies that there are many other temptations we face that are less obvious. What are some subtle tactics of Satan that are not discussed in the chapter?

5) Consider further how Romans 8:33-39 can help you to resist the devil in your life and ministry, and take some time to pray that the good news in that passage will fortify your heart against Satan's attacks.

Conclusion

The Leadership Moment

'In the world you will have tribulation. But take heart; I have overcome the world.' (John 16:33)

JESUS said that to a group of leaders-in-training, and it especially applies to those who want to see the church once again become a world-changing leadership factory and distribution center.

Regaining lost ground won't be easy, but the solution is simple: the church must follow the Bible's model for *defining*, *developing*, and *deploying* leaders while simultaneously rejecting the world's leadership models and standards. Simply put, the American church must multiply leaders who can transform the world for Jesus Christ. How can we do it? Obviously, it will require more than a couple of officer training classes or a few sermons on Christian leadership. The church can only become a leadership factory and distribution center if by the grace of God we return to both the biblical definition of leadership and the biblical method of producing leaders for the church and the world.

Instead of borrowing ideas about leadership from the fading world system, the church must make the most of this opportunity by defining leadership biblically. And because biblical leaders by definition are multipliers, they will develop more leaders – transformed leaders transforming others just as they themselves have been transformed, with each one multiplying and reproducing again and again and again. Then after the church has defined the biblical model of leadership and has begun developing leaders based on that model, we must be ready to deploy these emerging leaders into the world.

Every institution of our contemporary culture should be influenced by these transformed leaders, who will be armed with the Gospel of grace, the truth of God's Word, and the love of Christ. If the biblical model of leadership disciple-making is followed, Christian leaders will be deployed into every honorable sphere of society according to their God-given gifts, talents, and passions. If these new leaders are in business, they will incorporate biblical principles into their companies. If they are parents, they will produce Christ-centered families. Leaders in law enforcement and the military will understand how to protect those in their care and carry out their responsibilities with a biblical perspective. Christian attorneys will be prepared to advocate the cause of justice based on the historical Judeo-Christian worldview and will restore a once-noble calling back to a position of respect. Elected officials and other officeholders will be equipped to exercise biblical leadership for the general welfare of society, and true statesmen will replace self-serving politicians.

Contemporary culture would be transformed in an amazingly short span of time. The twentieth-century shift in American worldview from God-centered to man-centered will be reversed. What an exceptional gift of grace from the risen Christ through His church! But we cannot have it both ways. Either we lead according to the world or we lead according to the Word. Those are our only choices. We will either be conformed to this world, or be transformed, as Paul says in Romans 12:2. The American church can step back from the edge of oblivion and avoid the deadly freefall that awaits us. Or not. By the grace of God, we still have time, and this is an opportune moment in time. An open door is before us. The failure of worldly leadership has demoralized our culture, so the church today has been given a marvelous opportunity. By the grace of God, we can and must seize the moment.

There are two Greek words for 'time' used in the Bible, *chronos* and *kairos*. *Chronos* denotes the chronological passing of time while *kairos* refers to a season or opportune moment of time. The *kairos* leadership moment is now, and the church must not falter.

Our problem, as C. S. Lewis observed, is that 'Our Lord finds our desires not too strong, but too weak.'[1] The Word of God drives home that point with even greater simplicity in Philippians 4:13: 'I can do all things through Him who strengthens me.' Through the love of Jesus Christ, we are called by the God of the Bible to turn back the tide of spiritual disease and decay that now plagues our culture. And His leadership manual stands ready and available. The cultural death spiral can be stopped, and even reversed, by Gospel-driven and Christ-centered Christian leaders.

> An open door is before us. The failure of worldly leadership has demoralized our culture, so the church today has been given a marvelous opportunity. By the grace of God, we can and must seize the moment.

Remember, the church is called 'the body of Christ'. That means we are body number two for Christ. In body number one, He lived a perfectly righteous life, died an atoning death, rose from the dead, and ascended into heaven where He now intercedes for us. And in that glorified body He will come again.

During His ministry in body number one, our Lord Himself was a leadership factory and distribution center. He modeled 3D Leadership – He defined, developed, and deployed the Three, the Twelve, and the Seventy. The Apostles did likewise and produced leaders that 'turned the world upside down.' Now we, the church, are body number two and must intentionally do as our Savior did in body number one. We must commit to a prioritized strategy of multiplying servant leaders by defining leadership, developing leaders, and deploying servant leaders not only in the church, but for the world.

The church is not only called a body, but also a family and an army – a family of brothers and sisters in Christ who love their Father, and an army who is waging war for His glory. But one thing is clear: the church is not a business. We need leaders who know how to lead diverse body members into the harmony of

---

1. C. S. Lewis, *The Weight of Glory and Other Addresses* (San Francisco: HarperSanFrancisco, 2001), p. 26.

common mission and redemptive relationships (1 Cor. 12). We need leaders who are spiritual fathers and mothers to others in the Lord's family (1 Thess. 2:7). And we need combat leaders for the Lord's army who, like Joshua, are strong and courageous:

> When Joshua was by Jericho, he lifted up his eyes and looked, and behold, a man was standing before him with his drawn sword in his hand. And Joshua went to him and said to him, 'Are you for us, or for our adversaries?' And he said, 'No; but I am the commander of the army of the LORD. Now I have come.' And Joshua fell on his face to the earth and worshiped and said to him, 'What does my lord say to his servant?' And the commander of the LORD's army said to Joshua, 'Take off your sandals from your feet, for the place where you are standing is holy.' And Joshua did so. (Josh. 5:13-15)

Joshua's encounter with the captain of the Lord of hosts was what we call a 'christophany' – a pre-incarnate appearance of Christ – and on that day our Lord taught him four vital lessons about leadership:

1. The question for every Christian leader is not, 'Is the Lord on my side?' but, 'Am I on the Lord's side?'

2. As a Christian leader, I am never first-in-command; at most I am second-in-command, for the Lord is the 'Captain'.

3. God's battle plan will be foolish to the world (like marching around the walls of Jericho), but I should follow His strategy, for 'the battle is the Lord's'.

4. Christian leadership is ultimately an act of worship: 'Take off your sandals from your feet, for the place where you are standing is holy.'

Christian leader, embrace these four lessons as the heartbeat of your life and ministry. Rise up – blow the trumpet against the walls of sin; blow the trumpet of Gospel preaching and fervent prayer to see the walls fall down and men and women set free by the grace of God to the glory of God through Christ, the Son of God, our Savior and Lord. Yes, rise up, have done with lesser things. Lead on for Christ the King of Kings. The church for you now waits for you, your leadership and the leaders God uses you to multiply and mobilize for His church, from His church and into the world. Soli Deo Gloria.

Acknowledgements

I WOULD like to thank my Lord and Savior for allowing me to know Him savingly and personally and to serve Him vocationally. In that relationship, this entire vision for the 3D Leadership Dynamic has been birthed throughout many years. May our Lord be pleased to bless this effort as I gratefully thank Him for the enormous blessing of serving the Triune God and His church and proclaiming the Gospel of His kingdom.

I would like to thank Briarwood Presbyterian Church for the privilege of serving the Lord with you and for the encouragement of not only our members but also our elders, deacons, and pastoral staff – without whom this effort could never have been accomplished.

I owe an enormous debt to the diligent labor and untiring efforts of my ministry assistant, Marie Gathings, the consultation of Tara Miller, and to the editing work of Linda Waugh and Rod Gragg. Thanks also to Dave Swavely for his faithful and effective assistance in the enhancement, expansion and redesign of this edition.

To my family, I am forever grateful. My sisters Amy and Beth along with their husbands have been a constant encouragement and prayer support. Specifically, I would like to dedicate this book to my sister and best friend Vicki Reeder Hall, who went home to be with the Lord while this book was in progress. I praise the Lord for my children Jennifer (Philip), Ike (Angie) and Abigail (Ryan) and our 10 grandchildren. To Cindy, my precious wife, who is my ever present inspiration, encouragement, and counselor, I also wish to especially dedicate this effort. Perhaps more than anyone else she manifests the biblical concept of servant leadership. I also wish to acknowledge my dad and mom who now reside in the presence of their Lord and who taught in precept and practice much of what I later learned to know as Christian leadership.

In conclusion, to all of the pastors who desire to serve the Lord, proclaim the Gospel, equip the saints, fulfill the Great Commission, and see a Gospel-driven transformation of their church, their community, and their world, this book is especially dedicated. May our Lord bless you as you seek to first be faithful, by God's grace effective, and for God's glory influential for the pre-eminence of Christ. May our Lord allow you to lead His church, founded upon the ministry of prayer and the Word, to be a leadership factory and distribution center and together may we hear again, 'These men who have turned the world upside down have come here also.' (Acts 17:6)

Embers to a Flame Ministry

3D LEADERSHIP was born out of Dr Harry Reeder's passion for healthy churches because healthy churches must have healthy leaders. Spiritual vitality is a gift that comes from being Christ-centered and Gospel-driven through the power of the Holy Spirit. Other than the preaching of God's Word and intercessory prayer, there is no strategy more effective in developing a healthy church and in penetrating the culture for the Gospel than the multiplication and distribution of '3D Leadership'.

The ministry Embers to a Flame teaches the paradigm for biblical church health found in Revelation 2:5: 'Remember therefore from where you have fallen; repent, and do the works you did at first.' Out of the paradigm of Remember, Repent, and Recover, there are ten strategies for church health, one of which is defining, developing, and deploying leaders.

If you would like to explore further the ten strategies of biblical church health, we'd encourage you to prayerfully consider attending an Embers to a Flame conference. These conferences provide an excellent opportunity for a church's leadership to come together and work its way through the biblical principles of church health. During each session of the conference, an experienced church leader teaches a biblical strategy followed by group discussion and practical application.

After the Embers conference, the next step is Fanning the Flame, which partners with a church's leadership to help instill in the life of a church the biblical strategies for church health contained in the Embers conference. During this fourteen-month process, your coach will review with your leadership team the ten strategies taught in the Embers conferences, help make prayer an essential element in the life of your church, administer a church health survey that will identify the greatest area of need for your church, and most importantly, help your leadership instill those habits and skills that lead to a healthy church lifestyle. Your church will also come away with a written vision of what God has called your church to do and be in this generation.

If you are interested in participating in an Embers to a Flame conference or would like more information about Fanning the Flame, please contact us at:

> Embers to a Flame
> 2200 Briarwood Way
> Birmingham, AL 35243
> 205.776.5399
>
> info@emberstoaflame.org
> www.emberstoaflame.org

Biographical Data
Dr Harry L. Reeder, III

D R Harry L. Reeder, III is the Senior Pastor of Briarwood Presbyterian Church. He and his wife, Cindy are natives of Charlotte, North Carolina. They have three children: Jennifer Hay (Philip), Harry IV (Angie), and Abigail Leib (Ryan). Additionally, they are the proud grandparents of Brianna, C. J. and Mack Toomer; Kathryn Barrett and Anna Grace Hay; Matthias, Taylor Cynthia and Mitchell Elizabeth Leib; and Virginia and Winn Turpin.

Pastor Reeder began his undergraduate work at East Carolina University. After his marriage to Cindy, he withdrew in order to allow his wife to finish her BA degree in chemistry from UNCC. During the first year of their marriage in 1969, Harry was called by the Gospel of grace in Jesus Christ to a personal relationship with the risen Savior. After Cindy's graduation, he returned to East Carolina University. Responding to God's call in his life to the Gospel ministry, he left ECU and finished his undergraduate work at Covenant College, graduating in 1974. After finishing his B.A. Degree in History and Bible, he began to attend Tennessee Temple Seminary part time while serving an Independent Bible Church as a student pastor. Due to growing convictions in certain areas of theology and ecclesiology, Pastor Reeder resigned his charge in Chattanooga and went into a Pastorate of the Presbyterian Church in America in Miami, Florida – Pinelands Presbyterian Church – while completing a Master of Divinity degree with Westminster Seminary through the Florida Theological Center. Pinelands Presbyterian Church enjoyed the blessing of God's sovereign grace and grew from an attendance of 50 to over 400 during his three-year pastorate.

In February of 1983, Pastor Reeder was called to Christ Covenant Presbyterian Church as their founding Pastor. The ministry began with thirty-eight committed members and in seventeen years, attendance grew to over 3,000 during the Lord's Day morning worship services with a number of daughter churches being planted.

The Lord has also brought into existence a growing Bible teaching radio ministry entitled 'In Perspective'. The program is heard Monday through Friday on a number of stations around the country. Pastor Reeder also has a ten minute daily radio/podcast program called 'Today in Perspective' as well as five minute devotional, 'Fresh Bread'.

An increasing amount of his time is devoted to leadership development which has resulted in the publication of the book *3D Leadership: Defining, Developing, and Deploying Church Leaders Who Can Change the World*. In addition, Pastor Reeder is also engaged in conference ministries on the topics of Christian Manhood and Biblical Masculinity.

Pastor Reeder's passion for church planting and church revitalization led to the ministry of *Embers to a Flame*, holding national and international conferences each year. In addition, the *Fanning the Flame* ministry provides coaches for churches who have gone through the *Embers to a Flame* conferences and desire the next step of coaching. Pastor Reeder completed his doctoral dissertation on 'The Biblical Paradigm of Church Revitalization' and received his Doctor of Ministry Degree from Reformed Theological Seminary, Charlotte, North Carolina (where he serves as adjunct faculty member while holding the same status at Birmingham Theological Seminary, Birmingham, Alabama and Westminster Seminary, Philadelphia, where he also serves on the Board of Trustees). He is the author of *From Embers to a Flame: How God Can Revitalize Your Church* with Presbyterian and Reformed Publishing Company.

Along with a number of other published works, he recently contributed a chapter in the book *John Calvin: A Heart for Devotion, Doctrine & Doxology* for Ligonier Ministries in honor of the Reformer's 500th birthday. He also made contributions to several other books including *Statism II*, *Rulers* and *The Pastor Evangelist*.

Providentially, Pastor Reeder received a call from the Lord to become the Senior Pastor of Briarwood Presbyterian Church in Birmingham, Alabama in September of 1999 where he continues to serve a growing and vibrant congregation committed to its mission of *'Equipping Christians for God's glory to reach Birmingham and to reach the world for Christ.'*

FOREWORD BY HARRY REEDER

BIBLICAL CHURCH REVITALIZATION

SOLUTIONS FOR DYING & DIVIDED CHURCHES

✚

BRIAN CROFT

978-1-7819-1766-4

Biblical Church Revitalization

Solutions for Dying & Divided Churches

Brian Croft

There is a unique and special power and testimony in not just a vibrant local church full of life, but an old historic one that had lost its way, that was on life support, and into which God saw fit to breathe life once again. Biblical Church Revitalization calls us to an intentional commitment to church revitalization in the face of dying and divided churches.

Some books are written from ivory towers. Biblical Church Revitalization is not one of them. Brian Croft writes about church revitalization as one who has labored in the trenches of this work for several years ... this book is a "must read" on the topic of revitalizing churches.

Timothy K. Beougher
Billy Graham Professor of Evangelism, The Southern Baptist Theological Seminary, Louisville, Kentucky

I loved this book. Immensely practical and completely realistic. This should be a must read for all pastors and church planters when it comes to handling expectations of the ministry. Very, very good. Get on it.

Mez McConnell
Pastor, Niddrie Community Church and Ministry Director of 20Schemes

FOREWORD BY BRIAN CROFT

COLLATERAL DAMAGE

MY JOURNEY TO HEALING FROM MY PASTOR AND FATHER'S FAILURE

JAMES B. CARROLL

AFTERWORD BY CHRIS CARROLL

978-1-5271-0003-9

Collateral Damage

My Journey to Healing from My Pastor and Father's Failure

JAMES B. CARROLL

At twelve years old, James Carroll became the collateral damage of his pastor father's infidelity and his parents' divorce. With his world completely shaken and identity in shreds, he could hardly process what was happening, let alone begin regaining normality. In Collateral Damage, Carroll, now a pastor himself, presents the specific ways in which God has worked in his life during and since that time – healing wounds, revealing sin, and restoring life. This is a highly practical book, showing the gospel as the power of God to save, to restore, and to heal.

When a pastor like James Carroll offers counsel on care for the sufferers, you listen. When you realize that James himself has suffered, you really listen! Here's a book that proves 2 Cor 1:4; our hardships hold in store serious ministry potential. Heart-wrenchingly honest and immensely helpful all at the same time.

LIAM GARVIE
Associate Pastor, Charlotte Chapel, Edinburgh, Scotland

… a beautifully sensitive and moving gospel-biography that even [Carroll's] parents have supported. Yes, you will shed tears of sorrow over the pain of sin and its agonizing consequences. But you will also shed tears of joy over the healing power of Christ and the astonishing love of God's people for a heart-broken 12-year-old boy.

DAVID MURRAY
Pastor, Grand Rapids Free Church and Professor of Old Testament and Practical Theology, Puritan Reformed Seminary, Grand Rapids, Michigan
and Author of *Reset: Living a Grace-Paced Life in a Burnout Culture.*

Christian Focus Publications

Our mission statement –

STAYING FAITHFUL
In dependence upon God we seek to impact the world through literature faithful to His infallible Word, the Bible. Our aim is to ensure that the Lord Jesus Christ is presented as the only hope to obtain forgiveness of sin, live a useful life and look forward to heaven with Him.

Our Books are published in four imprints:

CHRISTIAN
FOCUS

popular works including biographies, commentaries, basic doctrine and Christian living.

CHRISTIAN
HERITAGE

books representing some of the best material from the rich heritage of the church.

MENTOR

books written at a level suitable for Bible College and seminary students, pastors, and other serious readers. The imprint includes commentaries, doctrinal studies, examination of current issues and church history.

CF4•K

children's books for quality Bible teaching and for all age groups: Sunday school curriculum, puzzle and activity books; personal and family devotional titles, biographies and inspirational stories – Because you are never too young to know Jesus!

Christian Focus Publications Ltd,
Geanies House, Fearn, Ross-shire,
IV20 1TW, Scotland, United Kingdom.
www.christianfocus.com